Everyday Life
in
Truro

Everyday Life in Truro

FROM THE INDIANS TO THE VICTORIANS

Richard F. Whalen

Charleston   London

History
PRESS

Published by The History Press
Charleston, SC 29403
www.historypress.net

Cover image: Pound Village (north Truro), circa 1875, drawing by Samuel Adams Drake.

Originally published 2003
The History Press edition 2007

Manufactured in the United Kingdom

ISBN 978.1.59629.364.9

Library of Congress Cataloging-in-Publication Data

Whalen, Richard F.
Everyday life in Truro : from the Indians to the Victorians / Richard F. Whalen.
p. cm.
Includes index.
Originally published: [Philadelphia?] : Xlibris, c2003.
ISBN-13: 978-1-59629-364-9 (alk. paper)
1. Truro (Mass. : Town)--Social life and customs. 2. Truro (Mass. : Town)--History. 3. Cape Cod (Mass.)--Social life and customs. 4. Cape Cod (Mass.)--History. I. Title.
F74.T9W46 2007
974.4'92--dc22

                        2007032056

From the Publisher:
This new edition contains the full text from the *Everyday Life in Truro, Cape Cod: From the Indians to the Victorians*, published by Xlibris Corporation. All efforts have been made to maintain the integrity of the original work, including spelling, dialect and punctuation.

Notice: The information in this book is true and complete to the best of our knowledge. It is offered without guarantee on the part of the author or The History Press. The author and The History Press disclaim all liability in connection with the use of this book.

Contents

List of Illustrations

Preface

This companion volume to *Truro: The Story of a Cape Cod Town* describes how people lived in Truro at four different times a century apart—around the 1590s, 1690s, 1790s and 1890s. It takes the reader into the home and workplace and describes the details of everyday life— what their homes were like, how they dressed, how they cooked, what they ate, how they raised and educated their children and how families supported themselves and earned a living.

The main events of the town's history are mentioned only when they happen to impinge on everyday life. Those interested in the historic events and trends may want to consult *Truro: The Story of a Cape Cod Town*. (The History Press, 2007) The notation (Truro, Ch. _) directs the reader to the relevant chapter.

Primary sources about everyday life in Truro are supplemented by books and research papers about everyday life in New England, and the authors of those works are hereby gratefully acknowledged. Their books are listed in the Sources. Additional details about everyday life from primary sources can be found in the Selected Readings. Many thanks also to Mary Sicchio, librarian in the Nickerson Room at Cape Cod Community College, a most valuable resource, for her assistance; and to Dr. Richard P. Keating, Natasha Babaian and my wife, Carol Pearson Whalen, for their close reading of the manuscript and valuable suggestions for improvement. Any errors that remain, however, are the author's.

Recovering details of everyday life in Truro centuries ago (however scanty at times the direct, primary source material) can provide valuable insight into the town's history and add perspective to our understanding of the major events, demographics, governmental actions and economic trends that make up the formal history of a town. It provides a new and more intimate dimension. The hope is that the two books—the history plus this companion volume on everyday life—will foster a greater appreciation of the nearly five centuries of Truro's remarkable history.

Chapter 1

The Pamet Indians, An Idyllic Life Abruptly Ended

By all accounts, the Pamet Indians were remarkably healthy, strong and happy, living an almost idyllic life for many centuries on the land that would become Truro. They fished off Truro's shores, gathered shellfish from its tidal flats, planted crops in its fields, gathered nuts, berries and roots, hunted deer in the hardwood forests and lived in harmony with Nature. Their food was varied, plentiful and nutritious.

Families lived in loose clusters of dome-shaped wigwams that could be easily taken down and moved. Favored sites for their sojourns in Truro were at High Head, Great Hollow, Corn Hill, along the Pamet River and at the end of Tom's Hill overlooking Pamet Harbor (*Truro*, Ch. 1). They may well have set up dwellings at other spots, wherever there were waters to fish, berries to harvest and open spaces to till.

They numbered probably in the low hundreds. When Captain Martin Pring and his men spent seven weeks at Pamet Harbor in the summer of 1603, Indian men appeared several times in groups ranging from ten to nearly two hundred (*Truro*, Ch. 2). The larger groups were probably Pamets joined by Indians from elsewhere on the Outer Cape who were curious to see the strange visitors from the two big sailing ships.

The Pamet men were tall, strong, swift and well-proportioned, according to Pring's narrative, which contains one of the two earliest—and best—descriptions of New England Indian people and culture (*Truro*, App.

Pamet Indians made their wigwams by bending saplings into an arbor and covering them outside and inside with mats made of rushes. Mats also served as a door and covered the opening left in the roof for smoke. The portable wigwams were easily built and taken down. *Drawing from* The New England Indian *by C. Keith Wilbur.*

A). They appeared to him to have darkened their skin to a "tawny or chestnut color," probably done with body-oil or paint, or both, over a tanned skin. They braided their long hair in four parts and tied it up in back, "in which hair of theirs they stick many feathers and toys for bravery and pleasure," according to Pring. Indian men had no beards; if any hair happened to sprout, they pulled it out.

Their summer clothing was minimal. "They cover their privates only with a piece of leather drawn betwixts their twists [thighs] and fastened to their girdles behind and before whereunto they hang their bags of tobacco," says Pring. Belts were of snake skin, moccasins of leather. In winter, they would wear capes of deer hide or other animal skins. English settlers marveled at the Indians' tolerance for cold. William Wood, who studied the ways of New England Indians, tells of Indians in winter wearing "a deep-furred cat skin, like a long, large muff, which he shifts to that arm which lieth most exposed to the wind." Apparently, the Indians did not wear headgear.

Pring saw only two women; he thought the men were "somewhat jealous" of them. The two women wore "aprons of leather skins before them down to the knees and a bear's skin like an Irish mantle over one shoulder." Other explorers and settlers in New England found the Indian women good-looking, graceful, well-proportioned and modest. Wood says the "women's modesty drives them to wear more clothes than their men." Although Pring was understandably wary of the many Indians he saw at Pamet Harbor since he and his men were interlopers on Indian territory, both he and Wood found them quite friendly. Wood called the New England Indians "kind and affable... rather naturally cheerful" (Excerpts in Selected Readings).

Pring, Wood and other English observers might have expected the Indians to be dirty and unhealthy because in their view the Indians were unlettered, uncivilized savages living a semi-nomadic life in the forests. But they did not. They almost always described the Indians as healthy, happy and generally agreeable unless they were provoked.

Their nutritious diet "contributed to a lithe and healthy body, vigorous and with stamina," says Howard S. Russell in his book, *Indian New England Before the Mayflower*. "All explorers who visited New England shores testify to this, and the English who associated with the natives after colonization comment on the great agility and endurance of the natives. An Indian runner could cover as many as a hundred miles in a single day, and on the second day afterward return in the same time." Their teeth, even those of the elderly, were strong and regular. Russell examined the jawbone remains of forty pre-colonial Indians and found that few showed signs of decay. Indian children were also in excellent health, exhibiting high spirits and vigor in contrast to the hard life of many English children. Too much freedom and a lack of discipline were the only criticisms made by early English observers.

The Indians did not entirely escape illness and injury, but they had a pharmacopeia considered more comprehensive than that of the English. They derived scores of remedies from roots, barks and berries—and the tobacco plant. Tobacco was used as an antiseptic on wounds and as a painkiller, especially for toothaches. Usually smoked in a wooden pipe or lobster claw, recreational tobacco was only for the men, and it appears they smoked the addictive substance fairly often, not just as medicine or a "peace pipe." The Indians' pharmacologists were not "medicine men" but elderly women who passed on their knowledge from generation to generation. In addition to drugs, the sweat lodge was a popular treatment. The ailing Indian sat in a wigwam filled with steam from water poured on heated rocks. Relatives and friends crowded into the wigwam and joined in chants and singing. Then they all plunged into a cold stream.

Most of the Indians could look forward to a long and healthy life, probably longer than a European's, according to Russell. Wood saw no Indians with birth defects and very few who were "decrepit." They were not subject to the many infectious, devastating diseases that plagued Europeans for centuries. Historians suggest that the Indians in North America were less prone to these diseases because, unlike the Europeans, they did not live in densely populated towns or close to domesticated animals.

A rich stew or thick soup with a variety of ingredients was the Pamet Indians' usual meal. Into the earthen pot went corn and beans and whatever else was at hand—squash, pumpkin or other vegetables, pieces of fish or venison, turkey, duck or some other game bird, perhaps some groundnut root for a thickener and sometimes roots of other plants such as the yellow pond lily or the Jerusalem artichoke (which is neither an artichoke nor from Jerusalem). The women had dozens of ways to combine ingredients. Their cooking oil came from seals and pilot whales.

In one form or another, Indian corn was in almost every meal, often mixed with beans to make succotash. The cook also roasted corn and pounded the kernels into flour to make a thick porridge or dough that was baked in leaves in hot ashes or on stones near the fire. She also made nut bread from walnuts, hickory nuts, beechnuts and chestnuts. Cornmeal from kernels parched in hot embers was their only food on hunting trips or when they were moving their dwellings to a new site. They mixed it with water or snow and ate it uncooked. The Pilgrims found a quantity of parched acorns in a wigwam on Corn Hill (*Truro*, Ch. 3).

For fruit, the Indians had wild strawberries, blackberries, raspberries, blueberries, cranberries, cherries, grapes and beach plums. They pressed them for juice, ate them raw and cooked and dried them for the winter. Although they did not cultivate berries, the Indians seem to have at least maintained the larger strawberry patches by weeding them and clearing around them. Pring made special mention of strawberries, calling them "very fair and big," and the Pilgrims saw "a great store of strawberries" on Corn Hill. Although not mentioned by Pring or the Pilgrims, there probably were grapevines in Truro. Indians elsewhere sometimes cleared bushes and tree limbs from encroaching on Nature's vineyard.

Pring's men dined on peas and beans with Indians at Pamet Harbor, but he adds that the Indians' own food was mostly fish. Fish and shellfish were in the pot or on the plate almost every day. The Indians ate oysters, clams and other shellfish raw, cooked in their stews and soups and dried in smoke for winter. In the Corn Hill wigwam, the Pilgrims found pieces of fish and some broiled herring. They also found pieces of venison, which was 90 percent of the Indians' meat. Other meat came from rabbits, raccoons, woodchucks, turtles, even skunks and frogs; also from game birds—ducks, geese, partridge, quail and the wild pigeons so abundant in those days but now extinct. If not put into the pot, fish and meat could be broiled or smoked.

The Indians had neither salt nor any sugar or sweeteners for their meals; briny oysters and clams put some salt into their diet. Fruits provided fructose. Their drink was water, sometimes flavored with the juice of a fruit. They had no fermented drinks, no wine or alcohol from grapes or corn. At mealtime, they sat on the ground and ate with their hands and wooden spoons from wooden bowls. They had no knives or forks. William Wood says that they ate "without trenchers [plates], napkins, or knives...impatient of delays... without scrupling at unwashed hands, without bread, salt, or beer, lolling in the Turkish fashion, not ceasing till their full bellies leave nothing but empty platters."

Although their food and table manners might have seemed primitive, the Indians' diet is considered to have been just as nutritious as that of the Europeans and perhaps better, given their physical appearance and stamina. Even without any dairy products, they had a diversified and balanced diet of protein and carbohydrates, which contained, says Russell, "all essential calories, vitamins, minerals, acids, and trace elements necessary for healthy, enduring bodies and active, ingenious minds."

In contrast to the popular image of the Indian with bow and arrow stalking a deer, the Pamet Indians were primarily fishermen and tillers of the soil. Cape Cod Bay was full of cod, bass and great schools of mackerel and herring that could be trapped in weirs. The men snared them with purse nets in streams and estuaries and caught them offshore and in Truro's ponds with a wooden or bone hook baited with lobster and fastened to a line made of hemp. They trapped eels in pots and weirs set in the Pamet River and Eastern Harbor. They harpooned sturgeon from canoes, and when the big fish were migrating up streams they caught them in strong netting. Wood says the shoals off Cape Cod were one of the best places to harpoon sturgeon: "Some of these be twelve, fourteen, eighteen feet long." An Indian harpoon point was found in 1967 in shallow water off North Truro's bayshore. It was barbed and made of bone, probably from a pilot whale. Fifteen inches long, it is one of the largest found in southeastern New England.

"There be a great store of salt-water eels," says Wood, "especially in such places where grass grows." The Indians caught them at night in traps they made out of osiers and baited with bits of lobster meat. They ate them fresh and salted some for use in winter. Wood did not think the

New England eels tasted as good as those in England, but eels would be a favorite dish for Americans until the late 1800s.

The Indians fished offshore from canoes, both dugout and birchbark. Pring was impressed by the birchbark canoes he saw at Pamet Harbor. He described one as seventeen feet long and four feet wide, pointed at both ends and with the bow "a little bending roundly upward." He said that although it could carry nine men, it weighed only sixty pounds, "a thing most incredible in regard to the largeness and capacity thereof." The Indians propelled canoes "very swiftly" with six-foot paddles of ash or maple.

The Indians could easily net the herring migrating up the Herring River to ponds near South Truro. Many of the fish went straight to the Indians' fields as fertilizer. Squanto, whom the Pilgrims met at Plymouth, would become famous for having taught them how to put a fish into the seed hole when they planted corn and beans.

Many generations of Pamet Indians harvested great quantities of oysters, clams and other shellfish from the flats of Cape Cod Bay. Oysters could be up to a foot long. The women did the shell fishing, using a large clam shell tied to a stick for a clam rake. Wood says that when food was in short supply the Indian women would "trudge to the clam banks when all other means fail." The Pamet Indians left large piles of empty shells in Truro. At High Head, some were three feet deep.

Deer—the Indians' primary source of meat—also provided hides for clothing, rawhide for cordage and bone for tools. They stalked deer but more often trapped them so they could get closer for the kill. The Pilgrims came across a rope snare baited with acorns and tied to a bent-over sapling. William Bradford unwarily triggered the snare and was caught in it by a leg. The Pilgrims also found a pathway, probably funnel shaped, that the Indians used to drive a deer to the narrow end where they could shoot it at close range from hiding places. To attract deer and make it easier to hunt them, the Indians regularly burned the old undergrowth in hardwood forests. The deer would graze on the new growth. The day before Pring left Pamet Harbor, the Indians set a fire that burned for "a mile space." He seemed to think it was some kind of threat, but the fire was probably a controlled burn of undergrowth.

Pring admired their bows and arrows. The bows were five or six feet long and made of "Wich-hasell" wood (perhaps American elm) painted black and yellow. Three strands of rawhide twisted together made a bow-string thicker than that of the English. Their arrows were about four and half feet long and were "made of a fine light wood very smooth and round with three long and deep black feathers of some eagle, vulture or kite." Their large, woven-rush quivers, a yard long and tapered, were decorated with diamond-shaped designs of red and other colors.

The Indian women did the farming. They planted and cultivated the fields of corn, beans and various kinds of squashes. Their tools were wooden mattocks and spades to loosen the soil and a clam-shell hoe for weeding. They had no metal for tools, no beasts of burden, no wheels for carts. If a wife had a baby, she worked with the baby strapped to her back. Older children, who also gathered berries and nuts, guarded the ripening crops against birds, deer, raccoons and other predators. Pring saw an acre under cultivation near Pamet Harbor. The Pilgrims noted five fields on Corn Hill that had been cultivated, one of them in fifty acres of open space "fit for the plow." No one saw any Indians in or near the fields; they kept out of sight.

In the spring, the Indians used fire to prepare land for cultivation. They burned their fields and spaded the ashes into the topsoil as fertilizer. To clear forest land for cultivation, they burned standing evergreens completely and spread the ash. In stands of hardwood, they sometimes girdled trees to kill them and let sunlight reach their crops.

In the fall, after the harvest, the women dried vegetables, fruits, roots and fish. Winter provisions were packed in woven bags and baskets and buried in underground storerooms lined with rush mats and covered with mats and earth. The Pilgrims dug up a basket with thirty-six ears of corn, "some yellow and some red and others mixed with blue" and a bag of beans. In their second "borrowing" on Corn Hill, they took ten bushels of corn from an underground granary.

Tobacco was the only crop cultivated by men. Planting tobacco seeds was a religious rite. The dried leaves, chopped or powdered, were not only a curative for pain but a sacred drug that was smoked during religious ceremonies and important social occasions. Pring noted tobacco growing with corn and squash near a deserted wigwam on the Pamet River, and the Pilgrims found tobacco seeds in the Corn Hill wigwam.

Their wigwam was not the tall, conical teepee of the western Indians. It had a rounded roof, like an arbor. The Pamet Indians made their wigwams of woven mats of rushes lashed to a frame of thin, flexible saplings, or limbs driven into the ground and bowed over to make walls and the roof. Mats lined the inside walls, too. The door, about three feet high, could be closed with a mat. In the center of the earthen floor, under the smoke hole in the ceiling, was the cooking fire and spits for broiling meat and fish. Around the sides were platforms and mats for beds. Their blankets were animal skins. Wood said the wigwams he saw "denied entrance to any drop of rain, though it come both fierce and strong." He claimed they were tight against the cold wind, too: "They be warmer than our English houses."

The Indians had dogs to clean up garbage after meals and to retrieve game birds. Whether they were pets in the modern sense is not clear. A dog was with a half dozen Pamet Indians sighted by the Pilgrims at a distance; the Indians ran away, they said, "and whistled the dog after them."

Not only did the women and girls do the farming and shell fishing, they also did all the work around the wigwam. Besides the cooking, they gathered the rushes and made the mats for their dwelling, installed them for siding and roofing, and hauled them to the next building site when it was time to move. They were the potters and basket weavers. They gathered firewood and fetched water. They butchered deer with sharpened stones and the edge of clam or oyster shells. They made the family clothing from animal skins. And they took care of their babies and brought up the young children.

The English were surprised at the ease of childbirth for Indian women compared to Europeans. Infants were laid in a bed of cattail, milkweed fluff, duck feathers or sphagnum moss. A mother nursed her baby for about two years and carried the baby strapped to a board on her back. Baby food was a paste of nuts, squash and perhaps ground meat.

Her husband and the young Pamet men hunted, trapped, fished and felled trees. They made stone and wood tools, fish traps and weirs, bows and arrows, harpoons, dugout canoes and birchbark canoe frames. (The women sewed the bark onto the birchbark canoes.) Indian men seemed idle and selfish to the English because they spent so much time hunting, trapping and fishing in ponds and offshore, which the English considered sports. Russell says "they were emphatically not sports but often exhausting, body-wracking, tedious tasks and deadly earnest," and, he says, there is little evidence that Indian women felt overburdened.

The Indians did have their sports and games. In contrast to the popular image of the grim-visaged Indian, they danced, played games and gambled. Pring described how they danced and sang to the music of a cither played by one of his crewmen. The Pilgrims at Plymouth also found Indian dancing noteworthy. Unable to understand its significance, Edward Winslow, a Pilgrim leader, compared their singing and dancing to the antics of English clowns. On his travels with them, he complained about their nighttime "barbarous singing" when, he said, they sang themselves to sleep.

Games ranged from an early version of lacrosse and something resembling soccer to dice-like games using stones, beans, small bones and bits of wood. Wood says they played their "football" on a flat, open surface of sand along a beach. The goals were up to a mile apart, and a game could last for several days. He notes their "swift

The Pamet Indians, An Idyllic Life Abruptly Ended

Indians dance at the center of this engraving, one of the two earliest—although totally fanciful—illustrations of Truro. The engravings illustrated Captain Martin Pring's narrative of his 1603 visit to Pamet Harbor. They were published in Pieter van der Aa's book, *Scheeps-togt van Martin Pringe*, in 1706. *Reproduced from the collections of the Library of Congress.*

footmanship, their curious tossings of their ball, their flouncing into the water, their lubber-like wrestling, having no cunning at all in that kind, one English being able to beat ten Indians at football."

A Pamet family did not "own" its plot of land. The band of Pamets had their traditional territory on the Outer Cape, and there seems to have been plenty of land and resources for all to share peacefully and without encroaching. Rarely did the early commentators on the Indians note any evidence of crimes against person or property. The Pamets were no doubt like the other southern New England Indians, who "neither secured their wigwams nor concealed their personal possessions, and had no laws against theft," according to Neal Salisbury in his book, *Manitou and Providence*. In addition to this remarkable honesty and morality, they were noted for their generosity and their sharing of goods and labor among themselves and with the English.

The Pamets were one of about thirty bands of Indians that were part of the Wampanoag, or Pokanoket, tribe, in southeastern Massachusetts. A tribe was governed by a sachem, usually an older man, sometimes a woman, who acted more as a coordinator, council moderator and ceremonial leader than as an autocratic ruler. The sachem governed through strength of character, ability to work with counselors and eloquence at council meetings rather than through physical strength or political maneuvering. The position was hereditary, sometimes "descending through the mother, perhaps to a sister's offspring," according to Russell. Nothing is known about the leaders of the pre-historic Pamets. In any case, they would have resolved disputes and made group decisions through councils of elders, both women and men.

The Indians saw spiritual values in all aspects of Nature, which was the great provider. They had various gods "to be pleased or appeased, not worshiped like idols," according to Russell. Their ceremonies were elaborate and loud as they prayed to their gods to make rain for their crops, give them success in hunting or cure them of illness. They danced and chanted and smoked their sacred tobacco. They mourned the dead with "doleful cries," according to Wood, and buried them with cherished possessions for the afterlife, their heads pointing to the southwest. The Pilgrims opened a grave on Corn Hill and found many artifacts, including a bow and some dishes.

Contagious diseases, advanced European technologies and zealous missionary work combined to doom the Indian way of life in New England. They had not built up immunities to European diseases ranging from measles and diphtheria to smallpox and the bubonic plague that the English explorers unwittingly brought with them to America. Their sweat-bath curatives perversely served only to spread the new and deadly diseases to everyone in the community.

The Pamet Indians, An Idyllic Life Abruptly Ended

An estimated 70 percent of the Wampanoag Indians died during plagues in New England from 1616 to1619, fifteen years after Pring's summer at Pamet Harbor and a year before the Pilgrims arrived. The remaining Indians had no idea that the advanced technologies of the English—plows, metal knives and saws, fabrics, guns, the wheel and beasts of burden—would overwhelm their culture so quickly and completely. Their belief in their gods was rapidly eroded by settlers who believed it was their religious duty to convert the Indians, teach them English and civilize them—that is, make them sober and docile citizens whose behavior would conform to the English way of life.

Greatly outnumbered by the newcomers from Great Britain who bought their land for trifling amounts, the Indians in New England were expected to quit their everyday way of life, which the English considered primitive, even savage, and adapt to the ways of the English settlers. In Truro, Indian grandparents in the mid–1600s saw their grandchildren abandoning their centuries-old culture under the pressure and attraction of new ways of living brought by the settlers. The Pamet Indians' way of life in what would become Truro disappeared in fewer than two generations.

Chapter 2

The English Settlers Carve a Living from Soil and Sea

For the first settlers of Truro, life in the Pamet lands centered almost entirely on the family. Husband, wife and children worked together day in and day out to survive and prosper in a remote land far from civilization. They cleared the land, built their house, kept the home fire burning and wrested a living from the soil and from the fishing grounds in the near-shore waters of Cape Cod Bay.

Everyday life on the family farm in the 1680s was quite isolated. The family had few neighbors, and those they had were not next door. There was no village and no store. No bustling harbor. No church bell within earshot. They were pioneers on farms scattered on a narrow spit of land projecting far out into the Atlantic Ocean and inhabited by only a dozen or so Indian families, who did not speak their language and whose numbers were dwindling (*Truro*, Ch. 4).

Husband and wife aimed for family self-sufficiency. They had married not for love but to combine useful skills, join in procreation and rear children who would help in the family's mini-agribusiness. Marriage was a business contract having little or nothing to do with romance. A young man or woman was expected to marry a strong, healthy partner of proven skills, leave their overcrowded parental home and make a living for themselves. Their parents arranged appropriate matches, probably hoping the couple would be compatible and even fall in love over time.

It was a hard life in unfamiliar territory, but unlike life for his relatives and friends in England the Pamet settler enjoyed

The English Settlers Carve a Living from Soil and Sea

a new-found independence and opportunity. He owned his land outright and could acquire more from Indians for very little in tools, clothes and trinkets. If he was one of the Pamet Proprietors, he had a voice in the partnership's decisions about the division of land, boundaries and rights-of-way (*Truro*, Ch. 5). The Plymouth Colony government was far away and generally left him alone. There were no tax collectors or military conscriptions. Life for his family was what they could make of it on their own.

Their landscape was primarily tall timber, both hardwoods and conifers, with white pines so tall and straight they were reserved by the king of England to be cut only for masts for his navy. "High-timbered oaks" struck the eye of an early Cape Cod explorer. Many of the timber stands were clear of underbrush, giving the forests the aspect of a well-tended park. The Pilgrims noted that the forests in Truro were "for the most part open and without underwood, fit either to go or ride in." The Pamet Indians had burned the undergrowth for easier hunting.

Records left by the settlers never mention the Atlantic Ocean; nor do those of Martin Pring or the Pilgrims. The shoreline—located at that time some four hundred feet farther east—no doubt seemed too bare, rough and inhospitable. The high, steep cliffs made access difficult, and the unbroken length of beach offered no safe harbor. The offshore sand bars were treacherous for mariners. Storm waves up to twenty feet high broke on the bars, rolled far up the beach and pulled down the face of the beach bluffs. The high winds and salt spray flattened foliage for hundreds of feet inland. The settlers turned their backs on what became known as "the backside," a term still used in Truro, although since then the ocean beaches have become one of its most valuable assets.

In contrast, the bayshore was not exposed to the often violent storms out of the northeast, and it had two harbors—the mouth of the Pamet River at the south end of Corn Hill and the wide, shallow Eastern Harbor with its narrow channel into Provincetown Harbor. (A tidal inlet in South Truro called Bound Brook was already silting in

A typical farmhouse when the town was settled in the 1680s or 1670s probably resembled this replica at Plimoth Plantation, although by then shingles were beginning to replace the traditional thatched roof. *Photo by Ted Curtin courtesy of Plimoth Plantation.*

when the settlers arrived and does not seem to have been considered as a harbor.)

The typical settler had a very large family in a very small house. Thomas Paine and his wife, Hannah, two of the earliest settlers, had fourteen children. In *Everyday Life in Early America*, David Freeman Hawke estimates that the average couple had seven to ten children, probably born over two decades, with about six or seven living on the homestead at any given time. The number was reduced by deaths, by boys going out to be apprentices and by older children leaving to marry and start their own households.

Home for the settler's family in Truro began as a one-room, un-insulated house with a loft for storage, where some of the children might sleep. The posts and beams probably came from the forests he cleared for farm land, clapboards for the siding and shingles for the roof from one of the many water-powered sawmills in towns across Cape Cod Bay. Boats with lumber could land at Eastern Harbor or Pamet Harbor. Paine built his house on the Little Pamet River, upstream from the harbor (*Truro*, Ch. 5 & 6).

A fireplace eight to ten feet wide, five to six feet high and probably built of locally made clay bricks dominated the room. Truro has an unusual bed of clay at Highland, which would have drawn itinerant brick makers. One of the earliest records mentions these "Clay Pounds." Lime for plaster could be easily made from the piles of clam and oyster shells left by the Indians. The shells were in great demand, and the Pamet Proprietors, the land development partnership, ordered that their use be reserved to inhabitants. Windows were small and covered with oiled paper until the settler could afford glass panes from England. If the family needed lighting, they could use pitch-pine knots or whale oil from pilot whales beached on the bayshore, both very smelly; or they could make sweet-smelling candles from the waxy berries of the bayberry bush.

The fireplace hearth was the center of family life, the hub of endless cooking and food preparation. The fire burned day and night. In midsummer, the housewife tried to keep it low so as not to overheat her work place but without letting it go out overnight. To re-light it, she had to ask for hot coals from a neighbor or strike a spark from flint and steel onto a piece of dry, charred cloth. On the colder days of winter, a big fire would radiate some heat into the room but draw heated air up the inefficient flue. The winters of the 1680s and 1690s were very cold; the winter of 1680–81 was the coldest in forty years. The family burned an estimated fifteen to twenty cords of wood, more than half

The fireplace hearth was the center of life in the home of a settler around the 1670s and 1680s. Shown here is the hearth in a replica of a seventeenth century farmhouse at Plimoth Plantation. *Photo courtesy of Plimoth Plantation.*

an acre of timber, every year. "Wood was America's chief resource, central to the everyday life of all settlers," says Hawke, "and all used it with abandon." Just a few years after the settlers arrived, the Pamet Proprietors saw the resource rapidly dwindling and prohibited the cutting of cordwood or timber on land they owned in common.

The principal piece of furniture was a table made out of a board or two laid across trestles or saw horses (hence room and "board" for servants). It was usually covered with a tablecloth. Chairs were rare. Adults sat on chests, benches or stools. Young children stood at the table to eat. The main dish, cooked in a heavy brass or iron pot, was served on a platter or in a large bowl. Dishware was wooden "trenchers" (hence "trencherman" for a big eater). Husband and wife often shared a trencher, and so did the children.

They drank their beer, apple cider, milk or, if necessary, water from a single large mug or tankard, or from cups or bowls made of wood and sometimes leather. George Francis

The English Settlers Carve a Living from Soil and Sea

Dow heard an anecdote about communal drinking from a man who visited a large family in a remote Massachusetts town that time had passed by. Dow's informant wrote that at the dinner table he "couldn't refuse the mug when urged upon [him] and selecting a place at the right of the handle, [he] drank, when one of the children exclaimed, 'See, ma! He's got granny's place.'"

Sources of fresh water were the ponds, a few springs and wells in low-lying areas that could reach the water table. The settlers could dig wells easily in the sandy subsoil but had to wall them with bricks to keep the sides from caving in. When the Pamet Proprietors set aside land for a minister at Highland, they took care to preserve access for all to "the best watering place," no doubt a spring there that has since disappeared.

Dining seems to have been a messy business. There were no forks yet. They ate meat and fish with knife and fingers, but they had plenty of napkins and tablecloths. R.B. Bailey found in the wills of twenty-three Plymouth Colony men who died before 1640 that "there were more napkins than any other single item in the inventories." Not one fork was listed, although spoons were plentiful. Earle says it was not unusual for everyone to eat from the stew pot set in the middle of the table.

Inevitably, sleeping arrangements were crowded and toilets primitive. They all slept on thin mattresses that could be rolled up during the day, unless the parents could afford a simple bedstead with a trundle bed under it for the smallest child. Older children might find a place in the storage loft. But the family had plenty of mattresses, sheets and blankets. Wills at the time listed generous numbers of them. Warming pans took the chill off the sheets in winter when the temperature in the house could drop below freezing. Mattresses were stuffed with corn husks, feathers or leftover pieces of various fabrics. Obviously, no one enjoyed much privacy, including the husband and wife, although no one could expect much. For a toilet, everyone found a spot in the woods or used an outdoor privy, if the family had one. Pigs rooted in the household garbage and other farm animals roamed freely in the yard. Conditions were quite unsanitary.

The women washed the family clothes and table linens every few months. They made soap from fireplace ashes and grease from cooking and butchering. It was an arduous process, leaching powerful lye from the ashes, then boiling it with the grease outdoors in a large pot. Earle says it took about six bushels of ashes and twenty-four pounds of grease to make a barrel of soap.

Their clothing was sturdy and warm and worn in layers. It was surprisingly diverse and colorful, according to wills of the time. Fabrics were mainly wool, linen and leather. Cotton was rare. Wool and linen came in an extraordinary variety of fabrics. Dow lists more than a hundred, including linsey-woolsey and a woolen called "everlasting" that was hot-pressed and glazed.

Men usually wore a loose frock over leather trousers and shirt or leather jacket. The frock buttoned from neck to waist and extended to the knees. A longer frock would be slit at the sides for easier walking. Shoes and boots were leather with wooden heels and could be worn on either foot. The round, flat Monmouth hat, made in Monmouth, Wales, was popular. A woman's nightdress, an ankle-length shift, was also her underwear, being worn night and day. Over that, she wore a skirt and a vest-like garment or bodice, and over that sometimes a pinafore or short apron. Her hat was a mobcap, a circle of cloth with a drawstring. Children dressed the same as adults.

A family that grew and prospered might add a lean-to on the back of the house for storage and sleeping and later as a kitchen. In time, an addition would provide a second room. Later on, the family might build a bigger and sturdier house. Thomas Paine, the most successful of the settlers, no doubt expanded his house in the Little Pamet Valley. He also built a barn for his livestock, a windmill to grind grain and a smithy for his blacksmith business (Excerpts from his will in Selected Readings).

Farming, animal husbandry and fishing put food on the table and clothes on their backs. The principal crop

The first page of the will of Thomas Paine (1657–1721), one of the first settlers and the founder of Truro. It is not in his hand but is a contemporary transcript for the probate court records. *At the Barnstable, MA Registry of Probate.*

was Indian corn, the stalks also serving as poles for bean vines. Squash and pumpkin plants grew amidst the corn. Their leaves kept down the weeds. Hawke calls corn "a miraculous plant, equally nourishing to man and beast, immune to most diseases, easy to raise—it took no more than fifty days a year of a farmer's time and thrived in a field of girdled trees—and easy to harvest." The yield was about seven times that of wheat or barley. "No part of the plant went unused," he writes. "The stalks served as winter fodder for cattle, the husks to stuff mattresses, the cobs as jug stoppers, tool handles and the bowls of corncob pipes."

Corn was so important to the settlers that their leaders voted to require each household to kill twelve blackbirds or three crows. They once ruled that every unmarried man must kill six blackbirds or three crows before he would be permitted to marry. Later, the Town of Truro threatened to fine every householder unless he brought the selectmen eight blackbirds' heads or two crows' heads between the middle of March and the end of June. The money would go to the poor of the town.

The corn/bean/squash crop was supplemented by a wide variety of vegetables grown in a garden in front of the house. Produce from the fields and the garden was dried or pickled for the winter months. The wife and children worked in the fields during the planting and harvest seasons, and also gathered herbs, roots and flowers for medicinal remedies that constituted just about the only medical care. That may have been just as well. Dow quotes a young doctor from Scotland who practiced in Boston in the early 1700s warning that medical care "in our colonies is so perniciously bad that excepting in surgery and in some very acute cases, it is better to let nature under a proper regimen take her course than to trust the honesty and sagacity of the practitioner."

Farm tools were simple and few. Spades, shovels, hoes and mattocks were made of wood with a piece of sharpened iron fastened on the end for a cutting edge. Axes and sickles were crude and hard to keep sharp by today's standards, and few of the settlers were very experienced in using them. Hayforks were strong saplings with suitably spaced and truncated branches. Or the trunk of the sapling could be split and splayed out at the end.

The successful family also produced modest surpluses to trade for manufactured goods brought across Cape Cod Bay

The English Settlers Carve a Living from Soil and Sea

from Boston, Salem or Plymouth, towns that had become centers of colonial commerce and importers of goods from England. By the late 1600s, more than a thousand ships of all sizes were sailing out of New England ports.

William Wood, who was in New England in the early 1630s, advised immigrants on the cloth, clothing and other goods they should bring from England. "Woolen cloth," he wrote, "is a very good commodity and linen better... and good Irish stockings, which if they be good are much more serviceable than knit ones." For the kitchen, he recommended bringing "all manner of household stuff... but great iron pots be preferred before brass" plus warming pans and stewing pans. Workmen should bring "all manner of tools," including nails, spikes, hoes, axes, augers, saws and iron wedges. Don't forget glass, he urged, adding that it should be "well-leaded and carefully packed up." Truro's settlers could acquire these and other imported goods through barter if not with cash.

Borrowing and barter were everyday aspects of the settler's life. If his fire went out, he borrowed hot embers from a neighbor. A settler who slaughtered a pig or a deer shared the meat with other families while it was fresh and was repaid later in meat, some other food, the loan of tools, or hours of work. With little cash circulating in the tiny community, the settlers relied on dealing through informal debits and credits to make efficient use of the community's resources. Farm animals were a major source of food and wealth—and trouble. Typically, an established, prosperous family had half a dozen cows and steers, a pair of oxen, two or three horses, five to ten hogs, fifteen to thirty sheep, several goats and perhaps a beehive. The animals ran free to graze on grass and acorns. The farmer was responsible for fencing to keep them out of cultivated fields. Free ranging animals were a constant source of trouble, and eventually town meetings would pass bylaws to regulate them. Officials called "hog reaves" impounded hogs not wearing a harness or nose-ring. Unsupervised rams were a problem in early fall, when breeding with ewes would result in lambs being born in the dead of winter instead of benign spring. At first, it was finders-keepers for rams caught running free in the fall. Later, the town decreed that an errant ram's owner could redeem it for a fine paid to the finder.

Cattle and horses caused environmental problems. Running free, they headed for the salt-marsh hay around the harbors, trampling the beach grass that kept blowing sand from burying the valuable salt-marsh meadows. The Pamet Proprietors were forever trying to get the owners of meadows to build fences. Cattle were branded on an ear. Twenty settlers registered their brands, called "marks of cattle," with the town clerk as soon as Pamet became the Town of Truro in 1709. Fifteen years later the registrations would total eighty.

Winter fodder for cattle and horses was corn stalks and salt-marsh hay. The native salt-marsh grass, which makes a nutritious if salty hay, grows on the highest part of salt-water marshes. This part is flooded by the highest tides— called the "spring" tides—that occur twice a month during the highest of the high tides. No doubt, the Pamet farmers became quite aware of the phases of the moon and the tides that made the meadows so productive.

Wolves were the largest predators the settlers had to contend with. Raccoons, rabbits, crows and other varmints attacked the ripening vegetables, but wolves killed sheep and calves. So many wolves hunted in the late 1600s on the Outer Cape that the community leaders offered a bounty for wolves' heads. Sometimes they nailed a wolf head to the Eastham meetinghouse wall. Later, the Town of Truro also put a bounty on wolves.

Cape Cod Bay was so rich in fish that the earliest settlers must have gone out in small boats to catch them, although details are lacking. Men and boys were probably out there with lines and nets hauling in fish to eat at home and to dry for use in winter. Closer to home, they could trap eels in the tidal rivers and gather shellfish. The English liked eel but reportedly did not like shellfish very much and considered them food for the lower classes. Lobster meat was fish bait. Pilot whales were a source of meat, blubber and whale oil. Men and boys drove them to shore by banging their oars on

the water, and from time to time the pilot whales grounded
themselves on the bay beaches and died (*Truro*, Ch. 8).

The main meal for the settlers was usually a stew of
vegetables and meat or fish. Meat, including pork, mutton,
venison and turkey, could also be roasted on a spit. Hawke
did not think much of their cooking skills. He maintains
that in New England "the daily diet most settlers lived on
was dull and tasteless, particularly in households that stuck
closely to the English ways of preparing foods. They were
not adventuresome cooks." He says they brought from
England "an ingrained distaste for vegetables." Parsnips,
turnips and other root crops they cooked into "something
close to a tasteless pulp." They adopted the Indian way
of preparing corn. They baked cornmeal on the hearth,
combined kernels with beans as succotash, and cooked
corn into a mush called "samp" for breakfast. They did not
like or trust the water, preferring milk from goats and cows
and light beer or apple cider, if they could be had.

Cooking was not only arduous and continuous, it was
dangerous. Sparks and embers might set the chimney or
roof on fire and burn the house down. The wife risked
having her long dress catch fire. In *The Writer's Guide to
Everyday Life in Colonial America*, Dale Taylor says that
"about 25 percent of all women were killed in cooking
accidents," an appalling statistic, if true—Taylor cites no
source. Giving birth was fraught with danger, too. Hawke
estimates that 20 percent of wives died from causes related
to childbirth.

The husband-wife partnership was essential to the
success of the family farm, and a failed marriage created
its own problems, especially for the wife. Abigail Steel's
husband purchased ten acres of upland and four acres of
meadow near Eastern Harbor in 1703 and became a Pamet
Proprietor. When he left her two years later, she asked the
Pamet Proprietors "to consider the circumstances of her
sorrowful condition (her husband being absented from her
and left her in a very low condition)" and lease her the house
and land. The proprietors agreed to do so for the nominal

sum of three shillings a year. The record does not say whether she had children who could help her on the farm.

Infant mortality must have been high, although there are no statistics from these early days. If children were born healthy and survived childhood diseases, they were put to work at an early age. Children as young as three or four had chores around the house. Until the boys were "breeched" at about six years old, they wore dresses like their sisters. They were home-schooled. Fathers taught their sons reading, writing and arithmetic as well as a farmer's skills and knowledge. Mothers taught their daughters how to cook, use the spinning wheel and run the household. There was no formal schooling by a teacher until 1715. Even though work on the farm was the first priority, children had their games. Taylor lists a dozen, all from England (none Indian) and still familiar today, including hopscotch, leap frog and hide-and-seek.

The impression left by the records and interpretations by historians is that the settler's family did not live as well as the Pamet Indian family. The reason may lie in their differing attitudes toward the land and making a living from it. The Indians seemed to live in harmony with Nature, keeping a balance between using its resources and conserving them for the future. Although seemingly primitive by European standards, their way of life had served them well for thousands of years. And for whatever reason, there was no population pressure on the land and its resources. Consequently, the Indian family, clan or tribe did not seem driven to secure tracts of land exclusively for themselves. In fact, they sold it all too readily to the English.

The English, on the other hand, followed the Biblical injunction in Genesis to "subdue the earth and have dominion over every living thing that moves on the earth." They came to New England to take full advantage of the natural resources, expand their land holdings, increase their stock of material goods and improve the standard of living for themselves and their children. This attitude and their large families used up resources quickly. Moreover, they were not as hardy as the Indians—they suffered from European diseases and they were at risk of being treated by what Dow suspects were itinerant quacks who might worsen their condition.

Whatever its well-being, the family "remained an absolutely central institution throughout the whole history of the Old Colony," according to John Demos in his book, *A Little Commonwealth: Family Life in Plymouth Colony*.

The family, he says, served many purposes, especially compared to the family of the twenty-first century. It was "first of all a 'business'—an absolutely central agency of economic production and exchange. Each household was more or less self-sufficient; and its various members were inextricably united in the work of providing for their fundamental material wants." It was also the "school" for vocational training and instruction in the three R's. It was a "church" for daily prayer and Bible reading. It could be a "welfare institution," serving as a hospital, orphanage, poorhouse, home for the aged, or even as a house of correction if Plymouth Colony sentenced a law-breaker or an Indian convicted of "idleness" to live with a family as a servant. Given the sparse population and remoteness at the end of Cape Cod, however, the Pamet settler's family had little occasion to serve as a welfare institution.

By the time the Pamet settlement became the Town of Truro, the settlers numbered about forty families, had signed up a minister and created a sense of community. They had carved a living from soil and sea, although at a price. Within two generations, the tall-timber forests that held and protected the thin layer of topsoil would be mostly cut down. Winds off the surrounding waters swept unhindered across the fragile landscape. The "excellent black earth" of the Pilgrims was parched into dust and blown into the salt water. Much of the treeless landscape turned dusty, barren and bleak, to remain that way well into the twentieth century. Farming became less profitable, and the town's inhabitants turned to offshore fishing and whaling to make a living—a living that was more adventurous but more dangerous.

Chapter 3

The Settler-Farmer Becomes Fisherman-Whaler

Truro's farmers became fishermen and whalingmen during the 1700s. By the end of the century, farming was a sideline for able-bodied husbands and their boys. Much of their everyday life was spent at sea. They fished from dories in Cape Cod Bay and sailed in small sloops to the fishing grounds in the Atlantic Ocean off Cape Cod. They shipped out on whalers that hunted in distant oceans. Some found work in the merchant marine. While they were away, their wives took charge. The women and girls, old men and young boys tended the farms, the garden and the livestock. They also did some onshore whaling and shellfish harvesting. From its beginnings as a farming community of settlers who occasionally caught fish for the table, Truro in the 1790s had become a town of sailors and sea captains with commercial links to cosmopolitan Boston in the newly formed United States of America.

"Not much attention is paid to agriculture," says the Reverend James Freeman in his description of Truro in 1794, "as the young men are sent to sea very early in life." And, he says, they were away for as much as two-thirds of the year. Shebnah Rich would recall the "excitement and variety" of sea-going life that attracted young men who could not "endure continued, disciplined labor from day to day on the land." Freeman notes that although Truro had no harbor of any consequence Wellfleet and Provincetown had "convenient harbors." Truro in the 1790s was the bedroom community for fishermen sailing from the two neighboring harbors (*Truro*, Ch. 10).

The Settler-Farmer Becomes Fisherman-Whaler

The Truro fisherman-farmer harvested boatloads of fish to be cured and sold in Boston and put on the table at home. One Truro native, Captain Robert Rich, opened a fish market in Boston. Freeman stresses the variety and abundance of the catch: "The bay and ocean abound with excellent fish and with crabs and lobsters. The sturgeon, eel, haddock, cod, frost fish, pollock, cusk, flounder, halibut, bass, mackerel, herring and alewife are most of them caught in great plenty and constitute a principal part of the food of the inhabitants. (Formerly the bluefish was common, but some years ago it deserted the coast.)" For this onshore fishing and local transport, he says, the Pamet River and its branches, the Little Pamet and Eagles Neck to Mill Pond, gave "water communication to a great number of inhabitants with boats, scows, etc."

He continues:

> *Besides these fish for the table there is a great variety of other fish, among which are the whale, killer or thrasher, humpback, finback, skrag, grampus, blackfish, porpoise, (grey, bass and streaked) skate, dog fish, sun fish, goose fish, cat fish and sculpion; to which may be added the horseshoe and squid.*
>
> *The cramp fish has sometimes been seen on the beach. This fish, which resembles a stingray in size and form, possesses the properties of the torpedo, being capable of giving a smart electrical shock. The fishermen suppose, but whether with reason or not the writer will not undertake to determine, that the oil extracted from the liver of this fish is a cure for the rheumatism.*

When Shebnah Rich was seventeen years old, he was one of eight fishermen on a boat that sailed to the Grand Banks off the coast of Newfoundland. When the captain found fish, the men worked day and night in two shifts. Standing long hours at the rail, they hooked fish on hand lines, hauled them up and tossed them in barrels. On Sunday, they rested, read the Bible together and sang hymns. "Sometimes," he says, "the monotony was relieved by visitors from other ships....I well remember an incident of this kind in July 1841." When the morning fog lifted, a big passenger ship was about two miles off. The ship sent over a boat with the captain and several passengers. "While they were on board," Rich continues, "the writer caught a sixty-pound halibut, as handsome as ever taken from the ocean." An enthusiastic Englishman "put his white, jeweled hands on the snow-white, slippery skin, exclaiming, 'What a magnificent fish.'" The visitors bought the halibut and some cod.

"I have pleasant memories of that Bank trip of twenty-two weeks out of sight of land," wrote Rich, who made it home safely. Just three months later, fifty-eight Truro boys and men were lost in the October Gale of 1841.

Everyday life in Truro changed dramatically during the thirty years after Freeman wrote his description of the town. Pamet Harbor became a thriving fishing port. Decades later, Shebnah Rich would recall how the "busy, bustling enterprise" appeared in the days of his youth:

Here were wharves covered with stores and sheds, crowded with vessels. Forty-nine were hauled up one winter, besides several in East Harbor [now Pilgrim Lake] and other places. Here was a shipyard, where for many years two and sometimes three vessels were at the same time on the stocks. Much of the timber was cut in town and drawn to the yard, all of which kept the people at work. Shipbuilding touches a host of industries. Three packets were employed carrying fish to Boston and returning with supplies for the outfitters, or material for the new vessels, besides several traders and coasters to New York and other points, which, with the hardy crews of fishermen going and coming, presented just such an animated picture as everybody loves to see. Salt manufactured all along the shore and the creeks and coves was brought down to the wharves in scows to a ready market.

When not mariners, the men and older boys were carpenters—building ships, houses, barns, warehouses, churches, schools, a new bridge across the Pamet River, a lighthouse at Highland and a windmill on Town Hall Hill. The windmill was built with lumber from a shipwreck that oxen hauled up the ocean cliff to the building site. The mast of an old schooner was the long leg that angled from the top of the windmill to a wheel on the ground almost a hundred feet away so that the top part of the windmill with its arms could be turned to face the wind. Young Shebnah was fascinated. "Inside," he recalled, "the giant shaft, the remorseless cogs, the iron spindle, the upper and nether millstones, were wonders of mechanism and filled my mind with admiration for the men who could construct such mighty engines for power and cunning."

He was also enthralled by the work of the miller:

> *He it was who climbed the slender, latticed arms and set the sails; he it was who hitched the oxen, waiting to grist, to the little wheel, and with the boys pushing, turned the white wings to the wind's eye; he it was who touched the magic spring, and presto! The long wings beat the air, the great shaft began to turn, cog played to its fellow cog, and the mammoth stones began to revolve. He it was who mounted like Jove upon his Olympian seat and with one hand on the little regulator...could grind fast or slow, coarse or fine, with the other hand caught the first golden meal.*

Rich was a relatively wealthy man, a merchant who traveled to the West and to Paris, and he no doubt romanticized his recollections of life in Truro during the time of his grandparents.

While fishing was providing more work for Truro boys and men, whaling in Cape Cod Bay was on the decline as a result of over-hunting during the 1700s. Truro's whalingmen instead found work on deep-sea whaling ships. Some rose to command whaling ships and own major shares in them (*Truro*, Ch. 8). They sailed from Wellfleet, Provincetown and Boston. Freeman says that "many of the [ship]masters employed from Boston and other ports are natives of Truro."

The everyday life of two maritime families caught the attention of Edward Augustus Kendall, a prolific British writer. He stayed overnight at the home of Captain

Obadiah Rich, whom he describes briefly as "an obliging, industrious and apparently thriving mariner, with a young family, a house, of which the dimensions were increasing, and a good tract of land." In contrast, he was appalled by the life of the family of a crewman on a whaling ship. A whaling voyage took the husband and older boys away from home for months at a time, with no certain day of return and no assurance they would make any money. They received meager shares in the profits of a voyage unless the whale hunting was exceptionally successful. Kendall was outraged; the truth, he says, was that the Truro fisherman-farmer fell for the promise of sharing in illusory profits— profits that were "both precarious and little" for the crew.

He paints a bleak picture of everyday life on the homestead when a family's men and boys were away on a whaling voyage:

> *The subsistence of all the family, young and old, depends almost exclusively on fish taken with a line, or on shellfish raked out of the sand…. In this pursuit of food passes their hours, except, when by the light of lamps of fish oil, they sit down to the wheel or the loom. Their persons are frequently squalid; their hair hangs often in dirt over their eyes; and their dress is marked by poverty….The land they possess, and which might be manured both with seaweed and with fish, is but negligently cultivated.*
>
> *The whaling voyage is terminated, and the men and boys return to their cottages. Do they come laden with the profits of the voyage?… Do they come to wipe off the debt at the store, and at least to begin a new account upon even terms? Far from it! I was assured by practical men, by dealers or merchants and by farmers who have spent many years of their lives on these voyages that it does not happen oftener than once in ten years that the shares amount to enough to relieve a whaler from his debts…. While at home, he digs for sand-clams and warms himself in the smoke of his hovel.*

Almost always in debt to the shipowners for his kit and rations, and without the means to pay it, he faced debtors' prison unless he signed on for another voyage. Rarely could he escape his debts, according to Kendall, who, it must be said, may have exaggerated the "squalid" condition of the whalingman and his family for dramatic effect.

The slaughter of a porpoise by a ten-year-old boy on the sand flats near East Harbor also drew Kendall's attention:

> *The solitary condition of the boy and the smallness of his size, compared to that of the fish formed a combination sufficiently remarkable to draw us to the spot; and, on our arrival, we found our fisherman, of about ten years, astride a porpoise of about ten feet long, in the middle of a sea of blood, collected in the hollow of the sand. Alone, and with a table-knife for an instrument, he was cutting the blubber from the ribs of the monster, a task which he performed in a very workman-like manner.*

The boy had been tending his mother's cows on a hillside when he saw a pod of porpoises struggling on the ebb tide over the sand flats. He ran down, picked one that was almost stranded, grabbed it by the tail and held on until the tide was out. Then he ran home for a kitchen knife, which he used to kill it. Kendall's traveling companion told him it "would yield ten gallons of oil, giving the little cowherd, at one dollar per gallon, ten dollars [a considerable sum] for his exploit." Like Kendall's ten-year-old, Truro men and boys would also butcher pilot whales whenever the whales grounded themselves on the bay beaches, or they would drive the whales ashore from boats by slapping their oars on the water.

Sometimes, men fished for striped bass on the ocean shore. Henry David Thoreau came across two of them: "Their bait was a bullfrog, or several small frogs in a bunch, for want of squid. They followed a retiring wave and whirling their lines round and round their heads with increasing rapidity, threw them as far as they could into the sea; then retreating, sat down, flat on the sand, and waited for a bite."

Another beach-front occupation was salvaging whatever came ashore from shipwrecks along the Atlantic Ocean shore. Although records are sparse for the 1700s, Freeman alludes to frequent wrecks and notes that "the strand is everywhere covered with the fragments of vessels." When word of a shipwreck spread through town, young and old dropped what they were doing and raced to the beach to save lives, if they could, but in any case to exercise what they claimed was the right of salvage to pick up timbers, cargo and other wreckage for their own use. While strolling along the ocean beach, Thoreau found boxes, barrels, a buoy with "valuable cord," part of a seine and a bottle still half full of ale, which tasted like juniper. He writes in his book, *Cape Cod*, that after some storms "more than a dozen wrecks are visible from this point [Highland Light] at one time." Inland, gale force winds in the storms swept across the barren landscape and blew in doors and windows. "If you would feel the force of a tempest," he says, "take up your residence on the top of Mount Washington, or at the Highland Light, in Truro."

Meanwhile, back on the farm the fisherman's wife took charge while her husband and grown boys were away on fishing trips. She ran the farm, raised seven or eight children on average, coped with diseases using only primitive remedies and dreaded the possibility that her husband's fishing boat would be overdue, then long-overdue and finally beyond hope so that her husband and sons must be presumed lost at sea. In her everyday life, she saw only a few improvements in the home and community from the days of her grandparents—chairs, forks, church socials and a greater variety of groceries and manufactured goods from Boston.

Farming did not produce bountiful crops for the typical Truro family. The topsoil that was not blown away was worn out. As Freeman described it:

The soil of the township is sandy, barren and free from rocks and stones. No part of it produced English grass fit for mowing; and it can scarcely be said to be clad with verdure at any season of the year. The inhabitants entirely depend upon their salt marshes for winter fodder for their cattle, which in summer pick up a scanty subsistence from the fields and swamps. The soil, however, produces Indian corn and rye, about half sufficient, and turnips, potatoes [probably sweet potatoes] *and pumpkins sufficient for the consumption for the inhabitants. Other vegetables are not raised in plenty.... The soil in every part of the township is continually depreciating, little pains being taken to manure it.* [Kendall says the favorite manure for corn was the horseshoe crab, "divested of its shell."]

The method of tilling the soil is this: After ploughing, it is planted with Indian corn in the spring, and in July is sowed with rye. The hillocks formed by the hoe are left unbroken, and the land lies uncultivated six or seven years [sic], *at the end of which, it goes through the same course of cultivation. Formerly, fifty bushels of Indian corn were raised on an acre, but the average at present is not more than fifteen or twenty. The soil was once good for wheat, the mean produce of which was fifteen or twenty bushels an acre. But wheat has not been raised during the last forty years.*

The soil is not only injured by inattention and bad husbandry, but also by the light sand which is blown in from the beach. It likewise suffers very much from another cause. The snow, which would be of essential service to it, provided it lay level and covered the ground, is blown into drifts and into the sea. Large tracts of land have now become unfit for cultivation.

A few years later, another traveler on Cape Cod, Timothy Dwight, former president of Yale, would write, "We saw a few melancholy cornfields," and hillsides that were "dry, sandy and barren."

Still, Truro's population continued to grow. "It has become full of inhabitants," says Freeman. From a population of 924 a decade after mid-century the town grew 43 percent to an estimated 1,320 in 1793. Freeman counted 165 houses in Truro, including forty at Pond Village, thirty-five in the Hogs Back area south of Pamet Harbor, twenty-eight in the Great Hollow area, and fourteen at East Harbor. On average, there were more than seven persons living in each household, which was not unusual. In his book on everyday life, Jack Larkin says that in 1798 in the Northeast "one rural house in five was occupied by two families." Truro's population grew no doubt thanks to jobs on fishing boats and whaling ships sailing out of neighboring towns and other New England ports. By the 1830s, Pamet Harbor would be a busy port with more than sixty fishing vessels that brought a short-lived prosperity to the town (*Truro*, Ch. 11). The town's closeness to salt water made mariners out of its settler-farmers.

Provincetown Harbor also linked Truro to the rest of the world. Many hundreds of ships sailed the New England coast, and Provincetown Harbor was one of the best and busiest ports with regular sailings to Boston and New York City. Even for shorter distances, travelers preferred to go by boat. Travel on land was slow and arduous, mostly on foot, until horses began to replace oxen as draft animals and for traveling. Horse-drawn stagecoaches would not reach Truro until the mid-1800s. Even then, the coach was no doubt simply a modified farm wagon with three or four benches under a canvas roof. In any case, as Freeman observed, "As the soil is a deep sand, the roads are universally bad."

The fisherman's house did not improve much during the 1700s. The typical house was still one room with a big fireplace, a loft for children to sleep in and perhaps an enclosed lean-to at the back. The more prosperous family may have had a house with two or even three rooms, one with a second fireplace for heat in winter in addition to the kitchen hearth. As suggested by Stephanie Grauman Wolf's account of everyday life in New England, the lean-to could be divided into a summer kitchen, storage space, and "a small chamber for the ill, the elderly, or women confined to childbed who might require attention." Dwight saw sheds or small barns for storage of salt-marsh hay behind many houses.

Larkin paints a dismal picture of rural houses in New England. They were often "much smaller and barer than it is easy to imagine today. Many homes were genuinely squalid...surprisingly small and meanly built, and dilapidated structures were often numerous." Sleeping

A typical farmhouse in Massachusetts around the 1790s. *From* History of the Town of Sutton, Massachusetts, *1878.*

was still crowded; children rarely had their own bed after they left the cradle. Mattresses generally were straw-filled ticks, although the parents might have an heirloom feather mattress, or later on, "live-geese feather beds," mentioned by Rich, that were filled with feathers that fishermen brought home from the coast of Labrador. These feather beds were filled with thirty to forty pounds of feathers. Warm bedding was essential on sub-freezing winter nights when little heat from the banked fire reached the sleeping quarters. Warming pans were in common use.

Winters around 1800 were especially punishing, and the sub-zero cold could be dangerous. It was six degrees below zero on a Friday in January 1806 when nineteen-year-old Ambrose Snow was on a vessel that was blown to sea from a harbor. His feet and lower legs froze and had to be amputated, probably when gangrene set in. He was engaged to be married at the time, and he wrote to his fiancée in Cohasset to release her from the engagement. As John B. Dyer told it a century later: "She replied that legs or no legs she would hold to her part of the contract, which she did, the result of her decision being seven daughters and five sons." Dyer says that Snow's "ready wit and unusual energy helped him to succeed," but he doesn't say how or in what line of work. For a century after, on especially cold days people would say, "It hasn't been so cold since Ambrose lost his legs."

By the 1840s, new houses might have two main rooms, and some were kit houses. Thoreau said that "the modern houses are built of what is called 'dimension timber,' imported from Maine, all ready to be set up, so that commonly they do not touch it again with an axe." Timber for the post and beam houses was scarce in Truro. Most of the trees had been cut down, and the wind-swept, barren landscape could support only stunted pitch pines and shrub oak here and there. Thoreau had to smile when the "brave old oaks" he had heard about turned out to have a "ridiculously dwarfish appearance...especially...the Liliputian old oaks in the south part of Truro."

The yard was often a mess. "A sort of out-of-door slovenliness," said William Cobbett, an Englishman visiting New England in 1818. "You see bits of wood, timber boards, chips lying about, here and there, and pigs tramping about in a sort of confusion." Archaeological records, says Larkin, show that some New England housewives "tossed broken vessels and trash out the most convenient door or window, and threw bones and food scraps into the yard to be picked over by their pigs and chickens." And if the family dried the husband's catch from the bay, the fish were dried on racks called "flakes" built near the house. Spreading the fish on the flakes, turning them and stacking them was women's work. Visitors to Truro found the stench powerfully unpleasant.

Small farmsteads like Truro's generally had no privies, also called necessaries and later outhouses. According to Larkin, "Many rural households simply took the closest available patch of woods or brush." Most New England families had a chamber pot or two for use at night and in bad weather, and, he says, "farm families often dumped their chamber pots out the most convenient door or window—sometimes, the archaeological record discloses, letting the pot slip as well and leaving its broken pieces on the ground." Garbage pits were rare. Inside the house and around it, conditions were quite unsanitary and unhealthy. Larkin surveyed everyday life in all New England and beyond from 1790 to 1840—his generalizations probably contain some truth about houses in Truro.

On the other hand, visitors to Truro who left records generally spoke well of the houses they saw. Dwight says that "the houses have the same tidy, comfortable appearance which has been heretofore remarked [about other Cape Cod towns], but are painted in fewer instances." Even Kendall says, "The whole landscape has much in it that is romantic. Night approached, and I passed some houses of respectable appearance." The impression left by Freeman, Dwight and Kendall is that despite its small size Truro's real estate testified to a sizable income gap between poor fishermen and the more wealthy sea captains and fish traders.

More than a century after Truro was settled, the women of the house were still cooking at the fireplace hearth. Wood stoves, the most significant improvement in the kitchen, would not appear until well into the next century. The wife may have had a "spider" and a "tin kitchen." The spider was a skillet with a long handle and three short legs so it could be set over hot coals. The tin kitchen, also called a Dutch oven, was a reflecting oven set in front of the fire for baking bread and roasting meat or fish. Aside from those small innovations, cooking in New England, as Larkin says, "had changed little in the preceding century." Cooking over an open fire was still dangerous and tiring work.

Rich, who had been a teenager in the 1830s, recalled kitchens with the nostalgia of a well-traveled adult for the days of his youth. He writes of "the spacious kitchens, always fresh and cool" of his grandparents' day:

How altogether homelike and hospitable were these roomy, unrestricted old kitchens, white-washed, floor-sanded and wide fire-placed.... The floors were scrubbed white as snow and sanded with white sand in puddles...Settles were a standard piece of furniture...with backs higher than the heads of boys, to break the wind and cold while the ruddy blaze kept all warm in front.

Illustration courtesy of the American Antiquarian Society.

...[The women of the early 1800s] *baked a nd brewed, washed and ironed, carded and spun, warped and filled, wove and quilted, laughed and sung, and rocked the cradle. They touched the spinning wheel and distaff with deft fingers. From the whirring wheels and shining spindle flew warp and woof fine as gossamer and firm as threads of steel.*

In contrast to Kendall's description of the whalingman family's fare consisting mostly of fish and shellfish, Freeman says families on the Outer Cape "cover their tables well with provisions." He describes a typical menu: "A breakfast among the inhabitants, and even among those who are called the poorest, for there are none who are really poor, consists of tea or coffee, brown bread, generally with butter, sometimes without, and salted or fresh fish, fried or boiled." A few decades later, Thoreau was served a breakfast of eels, buttermilk cake, cold bread, green beans, applesauce, doughnuts and tea.

Freedman continues:

A dinner affords one or more of the following dishes: roots and herbs, salted beef or pork boiled, fresh butcher's meat not more than twelve times a year, wild fowl frequently in the autumn and winter, fresh fish boiled or fried with pork, shellfish, salted fish boiled, Indian pudding, pork baked with beans. Tea or coffee also frequently constitutes a part of the dinner. A supper consists of tea or coffee and fish, as at breakfast, cheese, cakes made of flour, gingerbread, and pies of several sorts.

This bill of far will serve with little variation for all the fishing towns in the county. In many families there is no difference between breakfast and supper; cheese, cakes and pies being as common at one as at the other.

By "roots and herbs" Freeman probably meant the onions, turnips, pumpkins, squash, cabbages and sweet potatoes harvested from the family's vegetable garden and eaten fresh in season or from storage in winter. He says Truro women made their own butter in summer, but "their winter butter, their beef, flour, cheese, and beans, of which they make considerable use, are procured from the markets at Boston."

The housewife preserved pork or beef by salting slabs of the meat and covering it with brine. Salt to preserve the ever-present pork and local fish came first from salt works up-Cape and then from the town's many evaporating tanks (*Truro*, Ch. 12). From time to time, the Truro family also had venison, possum, raccoon and wild fowl.

Remembering the days of his grandparents, Rich admired the food, mentioning three times their brown bread: "Healthier and sweeter bread was never eaten than the substantial loaf made of native corn and rye and baked in the brick ovens." Also: "well-cured codfish," fresh eels, finfish and shellfish. For meat: veal, lamb, pork, "occasionally a steer or older beef," and chickens and game for Thanksgiving. Pork and beans was a dish for both Saturday supper and Sunday breakfast. The main meal on Sunday was a boiled dinner followed by Indian pudding.

The family ate at a plank table. Rich says that "pewter, or block-tin ware, was largely in use." Soups and beverages were drunk from bowls called porringers until tea and coffee introduced cups and saucers. Chairs were replacing the bench, stools and chests. And no longer did the family members eat meat and fish with a knife and fingers; forks were coming into use.

Alice Morse Earle cites rules for children from a booklet of the time: Children sat down at the table only when their parents told them to. They were not to ask for anything or speak unless spoken to. They were to break their bread in pieces before eating it. They were not to throw bones under the table or stare at anyone. Their main meal often was bean porridge and corn/rye bread.

The family drank weak beer and mildly alcoholic cider from apples. "Beer is a good family drink," writes Lydia Maria Child in her 1832 book of copious advice for the frugal housewife (Excerpts in Selected Readings). Her recipe called for hops, molasses and a pint of "lively yeast" to a barrel of water and grain malt. On special occasions, the family might make a fruit punch from a wide variety of ingredients—tea, lemon juice, rum, sugar, spices and hot water. "Americans drank...in enormous quantities," says Larkin. Cider was a common table beverage in New England, even for children. Freeman saw a few apple orchards in Truro. Larkin indicates that alcoholism in New England peaked from 1800 to 1820, when the Temperance Movement cut alcohol consumption in half, and water became the basic beverage, along with tea and coffee.

Almost all the water came from wells since Truro had no freshwater streams and very few springs. Freeman liked it: "The water in the wells, which is very little above the level of the ocean, is in general soft and excellent. Wells dugs near the shore are dry at low water...but are replenished with the flowing of the tide." He refers to the rising tide of heavier salt water lifting fresh water higher up into the wells. Tea was a political taboo during the Revolutionary War (*Truro*, Ch. 9). By the 1790s, however, it was back on the table, and a few decades later Americans were drinking coffee, too.

Although not much changed in the kitchen, the turn of the century was a time of transition for women in other important ways. Larkin says that "in the patterns of childbearing and the size of families, and in the rituals surrounding marriage, childbirth and death, there were the beginnings of dramatic change." By the end of the 1700s, marriage had evolved from the business contract of the settlers to a more personal commitment between a young man and woman who found each other sexually attractive. Sometimes the bride was already pregnant. Larkin says that in the 1780s and 1790s "nearly one-third of rural New England brides were already with child....For many couples, sexual relations were part of serious courtship." About this time, bundling became notorious as an amorous adventure in which an as-yet-unmarried couple went to bed together but were supposed to remain fully clothed. Whether or not it was practiced very often, bundling found a place in the lore of American history.

After the turn of the century, however, the pre-marital pregnancy rate dropped from one in three to one in five or six by 1840, according to Larkin, who called the shift remarkable. Couples reserved sexual relations for marriage, married later and limited the size of their families through various techniques. Unwed pregnancy would become immoral in the Victorian Age.

The wife gave birth sitting upright or even standing with the help of a midwife and women relatives and friends. Assuming all went well, they wrapped the infant in swaddling clothes. Then followed several weeks confinement for the mother. Miscarriages and stillbirths were quite common. Larkin calls them "repeated, routine events" for many New England women. And infant mortality was very high. Freeman provides a bill of mortality for the seven years from 1787 to 1793 in Truro. Thirty-four of the 278 babies baptized during that period died in the first two years of life—a death rate far higher than at any other time in life. They died of infectious diseases for which there was no effective treatment. In later years, they died of the childhood diseases diphtheria, whooping cough, measles and scarlet fever, even mumps and chicken pox.

In early childhood, boys wore dresses and slept with their sisters and perhaps with the servants. As had been customary for generations, they were breeched around age six or seven and sent to work with the older boys and men. Discipline was strict. Young boys and girls were expected to be quiet and obedient, to stay out of trouble and to take on household and farmyard chores as young as four or five. They were productive members of the family. "A child of six can be made useful," says Lydia Maria Child. "Children very early...can knit garters, suspenders, and stockings; they can make patchwork and braid straw [for hats]; they can make mats for the table and mats for the floor; they can weed the garden and pick cranberries." An orphan or a child of an unwed mother was generally bound out as a servant or helping hand to family that would provide food, clothing and shelter—a practice that continued into the twentieth century.

Schooling was intermittent, mostly during winter, and with all ages in one classroom (*Truro*, Ch. 10). For the family's school-age boys, fishing and farming came first; for the girls there were the household chores. They might find a few weeks or at best a few months for education after the fall fishing voyages and before spring planting. In 1790, town meeting created nine school districts with teachers drawn from the community who would hold classes for two months. Most of the districts probably used someone's kitchen-dining area as a classroom for the neighborhood, although some may have built a school or acquired a house for one.

Sometimes the classes were quite large. Thomas Fields Small, who lived at High Head near Eastern Harbor, told Rich that "he had seen upwards of forty scholars gathered in his large kitchen, where the school was held. The town was considering building a schoolhouse there." Pupils in South Truro could go to a private school funded by families in the neighborhood that was in Wellfleet, just over the town boundary. Teachers faced the challenge of providing instruction in reading, writing, arithmetic and perhaps geography at half a dozen or more levels of ability and knowledge, while maintaining discipline. Books, paper and pens were scarce. Memorization and then recitation, by individual and in groups, was an everyday routine.

The Settler-Farmer Becomes Fisherman-Whaler

Rich suggests that school was not all that popular with the "sea-going young men." He thought that three months schooling was "too long for some of these restless spirits that could content themselves on shipboard for months." Freeman, who was an education official as well as a minister in Boston, wished that Truro parents would take the education of their children more seriously. He noted that only four men in Truro had been to college.

The decades around the turn of the century marked the beginning of more convivial times. While her husband and grown boys extended their horizon to Boston and other ports on the mainland, the wife's circle of interest and that of her daughters expanded to include more women in the burgeoning community. Houses clustered in villages, particularly at Pond Village in North Truro and at Hog's Back near Pamet Harbor. Women in the more successful Truro families probably did more house-to-house visiting, perhaps sometimes for a quilting bee, local gossip and afternoon tea.

Truro's social life was also enlivened by the arrival of the Methodist ministers, who lured parishioners from the staid Congregational Church by their fiery preaching and more participatory religion (*Truro*, Ch. 13). The Methodists built their first church in Truro in 1794–95, and the town soon had its first church choir. A special town meeting appropriated $40, a considerable sum, for a "singing school." The choir, which brought women together for training and practice, was a success. In 1806, town meeting voted "$50 for the use of singing schools," even while refusing funds for regular schools, although educated-minded parents may well have financed their neighborhood schoolteacher. With a choir and a new exuberant religion, Sunday services were an occasion for socializing—the ultimate being the camp meetings during the summers of the 1820s that brought everyone together outdoors to be moved by evangelical preachers, sing hymns, join in full-throated prayer, experience religious ecstasy, visit with old friends, make new friends, eat picnic meals and sleep in tents or under their wagons.

The Methodist religious enthusiasm was part of a larger movement in New England that was called a spirit of reform. In Truro, parents got together to build a private school and hire a noted educator from Boston. Book lovers formed the first Truro library association. The better-educated men founded the first of several lyceums to debate the burning issues of the day. They met every three or four days at six in the evening. Their debate topics reveal a range of interests:

> *Is it important that males should be better educated than females?*
> *Ought early marriage to be encouraged?*
> *Which is preferable in the choice of a partner, beauty or riches?*
> *Resolved: that there is more comfort to be found in the single than in the married state.*
> *Which is the most beneficial to society, old bachelors or old maids?*
> *Resolved: that money has a greater influence on this community than women.*
> *Resolved: that it is wrong to take fish on Sunday under any circumstances except hunger.*
> *Which has the most time for the improvement of their minds, seamen or mechanics?*

The men could also meet in a tavern. There were many throughout New England, and Truro had at least one. It was run by a Frenchman, who entered history by overcharging Timothy Dwight and his son for their dinner. Dwight's son recorded their outrage in his journal. In a tavern, men could hang out, tell fish stories and drink hard cider, beer and "flip." Flip was a concoction of beer or cider with a shot or two of rum, to which was added cream, raw eggs, and ginger or nutmeg, and for a sweetener sugar, molasses or dried pumpkin. Recipes varied. It was stirred to a frothy foam with a red-hot iron poker called a "loggerhead" (hence, it may be, that two men were at loggerheads when they brandished hot pokers at each other). Alice Morse Earle says flip was "a dearly loved drink of colonial times...a truly American drink."

At the tavern, the men could also smoke tobacco or chew it and spit out the juice without offending the women. Isaac Weld said in 1795 that "everyone smokes and some chew in America." It would be almost two centuries before they would learn that smoking and chewing tobacco cut short their lives.

Death was part of everyday life in New England. Rare was the family that had not lost a child or a parent to disease, injuries in accidents, or storms at sea. Particularly dangerous for all were dysentery, pneumonia, typhus, typhoid fever, influenza and consumption (tuberculosis). As many as a fourth of all deaths in the northern and middle states were due to tuberculosis, according to Larkin. It spread readily among family members in crowded homes. Quarantine was unknown. In the spring of 1816, thirty-six people died of "the Great Sickness" that spread through Cape Cod. Physicians of the time called it malignant fever, putrid fever, spotted fever and the cold plague. It may have been typhus or perhaps cholera.

Towns with harbors were vulnerable to yellow fever carried by mosquitos brought by ships from the tropics. Gangrene and other deadly infections could result from injuries on the farm, on shipboard or during bitterly cold weather. And the only anesthetic for Ambrose Snow when his legs were amputated was a generous dose of rum.

Larkin's research produced a grim picture of rural Americans, who were "usually dirty and often insect-ridden" and who kept on working despite dislocated joints and poorly set bone fractures, "their teeth badly rotted, a source of chronic pain and foul breath to many." Pulling the tooth, the best treatment for a dental problem at that time, is probably the reason early portraits of the elderly often depict faces with sunken jaws.

Medical treatment was still primitive, "bleeding and blistering, purging and puking," according to Larkin. Child offers more than a hundred "simple remedies" for ailments from earache to tetanus, which is often fatal:

> *A rind of pork bound upon a wound occasioned by a needle, pin or nail prevents the lockjaw. It should always be applied. Spirits of turpentine is good to prevent the lockjaw. Strong soft-soap, mixed with pulverized chalk, about as thick as batter, put, in a thin cloth or bag, upon the wound, is said to be a preventive to this dangerous disorder.*

Folk medicine, however, was probably not very different from that of more learned practitioners nor was it necessarily inferior, except where surgery was required.

Freeman's report on the health of Truro inhabitants was more positive, but since his primary interest was topographical he was laconic: "The climate of the place is said to be favorable to health and longevity. Complaints of the nervous kind, however, are very common."

Chapter 4

The Yankees and the Portuguese of Victorian Truro

Portuguese was the language of almost half of Truro in the 1890s. In the schools, more than half the children were of Portuguese descent. At the Roman Catholic Church, the sermons were in Portuguese. The Portuguese had been moving into town for about three decades, and they would continue to arrive for two more decades. They found abandoned farmhouses for sale and fixed them up. They brought their own distinctive customs, dress, folklore, religion, festivals, music, dances and cuisine. And they established a reputation as hardworking, reliable fishermen and successful vegetable farmers. They manned the fish weirs in Cape Cod Bay. A visitor coming upon a farmhouse half-hidden in a hollow a few years later would observe that "the little gardens terraced patiently down the various grades will remind you of the Azores, and you will not be astonished to hear the farmer speaking the Portuguese tongue" (*Truro*, Ch. 16).

These Portuguese-speaking families were not from mainland Portugal. They were from Portugal's Western Islands—the Cape Verde Islands off the west coast of Africa and the Azores off the west coast of Portugal. Sometimes called "the Western Islanders," their contribution to Truro was described in a state report published in 1897:

> *They have very comfortable homes and are said to keep them in better repair than the former residents. They are mostly engaged in fishing and farming. They show an aptitude for certain branches of agriculture. They are not all confined to this village*

but have settled in all parts of the town. Wherever they find a cheap place for sale they buy it, and the women being industrious largely assist in the general support of the family. It does not appear that the newcomers compete with the old residents in the way of wages, but it is plain that they can live on a lower income and will thrive where a native would not be contented. It is evident that the native-born young men have gone to the larger towns, leaving their fathers' places vacant....In the southern part of the town, much the same conditions obtain as elsewhere, a large part of the inhabitants being aged, and as they pass away their places are taken by newcomers.

Most of Truro's newcomers came by way of the Portuguese community in Provincetown, which had almost ten times as many Portuguese. They were Roman Catholics whose everyday language was Crioulo, an island dialect of their Portuguese language. Many arrived on whaling ships that used the Cape Verde Islands or the Azores as a base of operations to replenish supplies and recruit seamen. For centuries, the two island groups had been crossroads of European and African trade. The newcomers from the Cape Verde Islands, off the coast of Africa, were mostly light-skinned Afro-Portuguese.

Even with the arrival of the Portuguese and their bigger families, Truro's population was dropping precipitously, and the decline would continue for another three decades. The old Yankee families were leaving town or dying out much faster than the in-flow of the Portuguese. In the thirty years up to 1895, Truro's population dropped from about 1,450 to 815, despite the growth in the number of Portuguese to 330. "There are many empty houses in Truro," noted the state report.

Provincetown in 1895, almost six times bigger than Truro, was about half Portuguese. Truro's Portuguese could hitch up the horse and wagon or they could take the train to visit relatives and friends and join in the religious processions on feast days. Mary Heaton Vorse described the festivities in her memoir of life in Provincetown. During the Christmas season, musicians playing Portuguese instruments would go from house to house at nightfall singing their traditional Christmas carols in Crioulo. A typical Portuguese family in Provincetown—and probably in Truro, too—would set a lighted candle in each window and serve elderberry or beach plum wine and holiday sweets to visitors who came to view their altar with figures of the Christ child, Mary, Joseph and favorite saints.

Vorse appreciated the Portuguese way of life. She describes the dark good-looks and self-confidence of the men, the women's colorful costumes and the generosity and exuberance of the Portuguese, young and old. "The gayest and pleasantest of all the dances," in her view, was the *charmarita* as danced by the old Portuguese at the Masonic Hall. In Truro, the Portuguese on special occasions danced the charmarita in the kitchen. The musicians played the fiddle, viola and guitar to make a bittersweet nostalgic music echoing the *saudade* of the Western Islanders—a sadness or longing for something hard to define. In his profile of the Portuguese fisherman, Jeremiah Digges says that for a Portuguese on the Outer Cape saudade is a "longing [so] acute that it hurts and saddens—yet he cannot tell you what it is he longs for."

The Portuguese family also brought new foods and ways of cooking to Truro. These included kale soup, sweet Portuguese bread, and sausages called *linguica* and *chourico*. The housewife marinated fish and meat in vinegar and half a dozen spices. A favorite dish was *jagacida*, a dish of lima or fava beans, onions and rice. In his memoir of everyday life in Truro, Anthony L. Marshall, himself of Portuguese descent, lists the ingredients for a dozen dishes.

The young and prolific Catholic families and the aging Yankee Protestant families apparently lived and worked in relative harmony. Nothing in the records tells of disagreements or friction between the two groups of different cultures and languages. "The life of the Portuguese and the Americans is more closely woven together in Provincetown than in any other place I know of," said Vorse, and the records suggest that the same was probably even more true for Truro. The state report on Truro said the Western

Islander "is frugal, industrious, takes readily to gardening, and the women are efficient aids in the maintenance of the domestic establishment....The second generation of the Portuguese are commended by the older residents."

In the decades to come, the two cultures would merge. Descendants of the Portuguese flourished and increased their land holdings. Young Portuguese and Yankees married and raised children. Portuguese surnames began to turn up as business owners and town government officials, replacing the Yankees. Some Portuguese anglicized their surnames or took Anglo-Saxon names.

Aunt Hepsey was coming out of the store in North Truro with an armful of groceries when E.G. Perry caught sight of her. "It was an odd figure she cut in that dusty road," he wrote at the start of his profile of this survivor of old Yankee stock. He had met her off-Cape and promised himself to see her again when he was in Truro researching for his book, *A Trip Around Cape Cod* (1898).

> *She was dressed in a blue woolen gown, which reached low to the feet, and what was once called a 'poke' or 'coal scuttle' bonnet of yellow straw, adorned only with black, velvet strings and noticeable for its great size....Her shoes were probably brogans, although her long dress prevented certainty....She seemed a strongly built woman of past middle age...with blue, friendly eyes.* [Her face was] *tanned and wrinkled* [but in her youth she might have been] *a fair-haired blonde with roses, dimmed by the sun, in her cheeks.*

Hepsey was short for Hepsibah, a Biblical name. Perry does not give her last name.

Aunt Hepsey, he says, "was indeed a character. First, she was aunt to the whole town, and especially the children... who knew her by no other name." She was a regular at christenings, and once "stood sponsor for the son of a colored seaman away on the Banks for fish." The name written in the parish register was simply "Aunt Hepsey," although it was later replaced by her full name. She had a special feeling for seamen. Perry reports that as family members left town and died out she alone occupied the family pew in the meetinghouse "except for the strange seamen she insisted should be put there."

She assisted at half the births in town. "She was acquainted with all medical herbs," says Perry, "and was often on hand and administering when the doctor was not. Her medical diploma and skill (and she had both) were deserved by her long serving."

Aunt Hepsey was a great favorite of the girls. She was "milliner and matchmaker," helping them with their clothes and counseling them on their love lives. In turn, they once tried to help her to dress more fashionably for church, including a straw sailor's hat, long white gloves and new shoes. But no one could find gloves to fit her arms, and her feet could not tolerate the new shoes. She went to church once in her new short-sleeved dress and straw hat but gloveless and wearing her everyday brogans. The next Sunday she wore her usual outfit, including the big coal-scuttle bonnet.

She was addicted to snuff. She kept it in a silver snuff-box with the initials "J. A." and inhaled it through her nose. It was "the yellow kind and not over-perfumed, real tobacco," according to Perry, who calls tobacco her only fault. When he asked her whose initials were on the box, she refused to answer and went out to feed the chickens. A friend later told him why. The snuff-box was a gift years ago from Job Atkins, her sweetheart, who perished on a fishing trip to the Newfoundland Banks.

Living with Aunt Hepsey was her niece, who had lost her mind and was known as Crazy Jane. Aunt Hepsey told Perry her story: Jane and Harry Lumbert were engaged to be married. On the night before he left on a fishing trip, she begged him not to go; something told her he wouldn't return. He promised he would, and with enough money to buy the field behind their house. His ship never returned, and none of the crew was ever heard from again. Two years later, Jane was still waiting, her wedding dress spread in her bedroom. She stopped talking to people. Her wedding dress, turning yellow, was now in Aunt Hepsey's spare bedroom. Perhaps the ill-fated loves of the aunt and her niece explain Aunt Hepsey's invitation to seamen to join her in her meetinghouse pew.

Reminders of the perils of the sea were all around her. Her hired man, Portuguese Joe, was saved from drowning by her father during a fishing trip and ever after was loyal to him and then to his farm and daughter. Their dog, Foxy, had a peculiar aversion to water especially the ocean, reportedly, according to Perry, because his mother had been washed ashore from a ship at sea.

Perry describes Aunt Hepsey's house as typical of Cape Cod at the time, shingled with a chimney in the center, two rooms in front and the long kitchen at the back running "the whole width of the house, with closets, butteries and bedrooms at either end of it" and with a huge open fireplace at the center. Under the roof were two sleeping chambers, where Hepsey slept in her youth, and "where the wind blew through some slight snow in the stormier winter nights."

"The floor of the big kitchen was as white and clean as sand and scouring could make it," says Perry. When Aunt Hepsey fell asleep in front of the fire, probably during a lull in their conversation, Perry took note of her wooden trenchers, pewter porringers and platters, and "her choice table crockery."

Victorian America was a time of migration, modernism and growth. Thomas J. Schlereth says in his book *Victorian America: Transformations in Everyday Life*, 1876–1915 that "migration, movement, and mobility accelerated enormously." Everybody seemed to be on the move, relocating and resettling, leaving the farm for the city and the city for the wide-open West, while immigrants were arriving from Europe. It was a time of technological advances, economic growth and a fascination with material goods. New technologies made dramatic changes in the workplace, housing, food preparation, consumer goods, education, recreation, transportation and communications.

The Yankees and the Portuguese of Victorian Truro

Among the leading forces for change were the railroad and the telegraph.

Everyday life in Truro, however, did not share in the economic growth and prosperity. Its population was declining rapidly, and its economy—if a town of less than a thousand could be said to have an economy—was unexceptional. Many houses and farms were abandoned. Ambitious men and women for decades had been moving to Boston, among them men from the Freeman, Avery and Rich families who became prominent merchants there. They and others bought houses in Boston and especially suburban Somerville. Shebnah Rich, who was one of them, said in the 1880s that "over one hundred families from Truro now reside in Somerville."

The elderly poor were left behind. Recalling those days around the turn of the century, Marshall says it was always a mystery to him "how some of the older people and the retired eked out a living." If they had no family left to support them, they went to the town poorhouse. Funding to support ten to fifteen of the poor was a major item in the town budget. The amount, which varied from year to year, ranged from a quarter to almost half of the school budget. After the poorhouse closed in 1896, the town's overseers of the poor disbursed funds to support as many as twenty men and women living in poorhouses from Wellfleet to Newburyport.

In some ways, however, life in Truro was influenced by Victorian mobility and modernism and even by the spirit of the Gay Nineties. Immigrants from the Western Islands and their descendants moved in and replaced long-established Yankee families. New technologies transformed fish processing and brought a radical change to the kitchen. The railroad brought coal, manufactured goods and vacationers to Truro and offered its younger people transportation to the big cities and the West. The telegraph made Truro an important marine reporting station where a shipping monitor near Highland Light used a telescope and telegraph key to alert Boston merchants that cargo ships were approaching port. A Truro resident could buy newspapers from Provincetown, Wellfleet or Barnstable, all carrying advertising for the latest conveniences and material goods.

The most significant household convenience was the cast iron cookstove. It was the dominant feature of everyday domestic life in the second half of the 1900s in America, although the housewife often had ambiguous feelings about it. On Cape Cod, probate records at mid-century show that more than half the estate inventories included cookstoves. They were found in both modest and wealthy households. (Aunt Hepsey apparently was among those who had not yet bought one.)

Americans were ambivalent about cookstoves. Everyone wanted to get away from the hot, dangerous, awkward cooking at the fireplace hearth, while at the same time regretting the loss of traditional family life at the hearth. A nostalgia for the good old days arrived with delivery of the eagerly awaited cast iron cookstove. Shebnah Rich in the 1880s voiced a poignant nostalgia for the old days before cookstoves and said some households were even "returning to the wood fire, blazing and crackling on the open hearth," but probably not for cooking. A fireplace in the front parlor could replace the kitchen fireplace for domestic warmth and cheer, although cast iron parlor stoves were also for sale.

Cookstoves raised expectations that could not be fulfilled. Widespread advertising led women to believe that a cookstove would be easy to use and clean. It did keep the fire enclosed, heating more evenly and saving wood or coal, and it raised the cooking surface from the hearth to waist level. But manufacturers produced a bewildering array of cookstoves, hundreds of them, plus a range of attachments. Many were elaborately designed and ornamented, some hardly resembling a stove for cooking. Some were seriously flawed in their functional design. Each required special skills and attention to its draft and damper controls. The hidden fire was cantankerous and difficult to adjust. Back drafts blew clouds of smoke into the kitchen. Different woods and coal produced different results. Coal fires were hard

"It Won't Draw. It Just Smokes." The title of this drawing from a book published in 1870 sums up one of the challenges of the cast iron cookstove. It may have been an improvement over cooking at the fireplace hearth, but it had its drawbacks. *From* What She Could, *by Susan Warner.*

to start and emitted noxious fumes if not properly vented. And greasy soot had to be cleaned from the stovepipes. At the same time, the housewife struggling with her cookstove could read about the promise of the wonderful convenience of gas and electric stoves that were being developed.

The kitchen was the center of family life, especially for the Portuguese. The women did their sewing and ironing at the kitchen table, where the family ate their meals. They washed clothes and linens on a corrugated washboard and put them through a hand-cranked wringer. With the cookstove replacing fireplace flames, light came from candles, whale oil lamps or kerosene lamps. These could be lighted by friction matches, which were just coming into everyday use. Well water was hauled up in a bucket, pumped up by hand or pumped into a tank by a windmill, which was becoming a common feature of Truro's landscape. Some homes had a cistern to collect rainwater from the roof. Dirty water from the kitchen sink or bathing was dumped outside. Kitchen garbage was also dumped outside either into a pit or into the backyard for the pigs.

The family ate fish and shellfish from Cape Cod Bay and the Pamet River, fruit and vegetables from their garden, chicken and eggs from the barnyard, milk from cows, salted or marinated pork and beef, Portuguese soups and sausages and fresh meat at slaughtering time. Iceboxes began to appear in some homes. Cold winters around the turn of the century produced thick ice on the ponds. Stored in underground or insulated icehouses, pond ice was used to preserve fish during shipment, and some of it must have found its way into the home. Meals were heavy and eaten in a hurry. Most foods, even vegetables, were fried in lard, bacon grease or butter. "Dyspepsia, or indigestion, was the most universal physical complaint of the nineteenth century," says Daniel E. Sutherland in his book on everyday life in the late 1800s.

Few Truro families, if any, built new houses. There were plenty of abandoned houses, many of them built during the pre-Civil War boom. None had plumbing; all had an outhouse, or privy, in the backyard. Bedrooms usually had a basin and water pitcher. The farmer, his sons and the farm help washed before meals in a tub outside the back door. Many even took a full bath in warm water in the kitchen every month or two. The successful family would have a barn for horses and cows, a woodshed and a chicken coop. They might add a wing to the house or build a summerhouse for cooking and laundering during the hot summer months. In any case, there was no special architectural style for farmhouses in the late 1800s.

As Truro's offshore fishing industry collapsed and the town's population shrank in the second half of the 1800s, the husband and wife who stayed in town found a variety of other ways to support their family, although much of it was part-time. No single occupation, such as farming or fishing, could describe the everyday life of the typical Truro family of the 1890s. Husband, wife and older children found work in weir fishing, processing fish, dairy farming, raising vegetables and chickens, cranberry farming, picking wild berries and fruit from orchards, teaching school, operating stores, working at the summer resorts, on the railroad, on town road maintenance and improvements and in the U.S. Life-Saving Service. In contrast to earlier times when most people were largely self-sufficient or worked for shares, more and more men and women were on a payroll, whether for the weir fishing companies, the railroad, the resorts, the town or the federal government.

The days were long gone when nearly every able-bodied boy and man called himself a fisherman, but weir fishing provided work for about a hundred men, almost all of them Portuguese. During the fishing season, the tops of slender poles holding the nets speckled the Cape Cod Bay shoreline from one end of Truro to the other. The 1897 state report observed: "The principal industry in the town of Truro is fishing. There is a cold storage plant at North Truro, but weirs and traps, with a little fishing from the shore, are the principal source of income. The catching of eels in fyke nets...has recently become of some importance." ("Fyke" was a Dutch word for a bag net.) Eels were a popular dish.

Fifteen men took out licenses to trap eels in the Pamet rivers in 1897. Besides working on the fish weirs, some Portuguese men undoubtedly found work on offshore fishing boats and whalers based in Provincetown.

The town's entrepreneur, Captain Atkins Hughes, a retired clipper ship captain, invested in fish weirs in 1893 and raised the capital to build a cold storage plant on the railroad line in North Truro. When the fish were running, there were jobs processing fish in the plant and for a few years around the turn of the century at a fish canning factory in North Truro.

Provincetown was the principal market for the housewife's surplus fruit, vegetables, chickens, eggs and especially milk. In her book on Cape Cod, Katherine Crosby reports a jeering rhyme:

> *Provincetown for beauty,*
> *Wellfleet for her pride—*
> *If it hadn't been for milk carts,*
> *Truro would've died*

Dairy products were a third of Truro's home-based agriculture. A census counted 211 cows in 1902. Poultry products and vegetables following with each at about 18 percent of the total, according to the state report. Truro's turnips were supposed to be especially good.

Vegetable gardens flourished in patches of boggy ground and wherever fresh water could be found. The state report said: "At North Truro what was once a large pond or swamp has been filled in quite extensively from time to time. It has proved a good meadow and maintains vegetable gardens in dry season. Part of this was made into cranberry bogs with fair success." Vegetable gardens appeared at the bottom of hollows where the soil was richer and along the Upper Pamet River. The dike across the Pamet River in Truro Center stopped salt water from reaching the Upper Pamet and destroyed the salt marsh hay meadows there, but fresh water from the water table made it good for gardening. According to the state report:

The Yankees and the Portuguese of Victorian Truro

In investigations upon the Pamet River, it was found that the dike [in Truro Center] *was built in 1869 by the town of Truro for a highway, in place of the old wooden bridge. Its effect upon the salt meadow is said to be unfavorable, as this meadow is now over-run with flags* [cattails]. *The river banks, however, and some of the upper meadows have been made into fine gardens, which even in dry seasons do well. Some of the marsh has been turned into cranberry bogs, but they were not a success. On the south bank of this river above the dike the soil is considered good, and most of these places are occupied by the Western Islanders.*

By the 1890s, cultivating cranberries for market was a major industry on Cape Cod. Farmers who had a bog on their property or who could flood a lowland with fresh water went into the business. The largest cranberry bogs in Truro were in Great Swamp (now called Shearwater) and near the end of North Pamet Road, a bog that is now in the Cape Cod National Seashore, which has restored the bog house there (*Truro*, Ch. 16).

Operating a cranberry bog was not full-time work, but there was work to be done at almost every season. The cranberry plants were trimmed in the late fall, weeded late the next spring, covered lightly with sand in the summer and harvested in September and October. The harvest workers were mostly women and children. Because of high absenteeism in the schools those two months, classes started late in the fall for a few years to allow the schoolchildren to join in the harvesting. Around the turn of the century, the growers began to hire Cape Verdean men and women from out of town. The harvesters picked the berries by hand and later used wide, varnished-wood scoops with teeth at the front end to pull the berries from the vines. Women sorted and cleaned the berries and packed them for shipment by train. After the harvest, gleaners could scour the bogs for berries they could keep.

After the late fall trimming, the farmer flooded the bog to wash out the leaves, dead vines and other debris and to protect the vines from winter-kill. Charlie Snow told

Picking and sorting cranberries was work for women and children. This drawing of the harvest on Outer Cape Cod suggests the landscape of the Upper Pamet Valley. *By Samuel Adams Drake in his* Nooks and Corners of New England, *1875.*

newspaper columnist Tom Kane how he was hired to get "the big one-lung gas engine a-goin' and put the pump to workin' and flood the bog." To start it, he attached about six batteries to the magneto system "to hotten up the spark." Then he heated the glow plug, screwed it into the engine's cylinder and turned the fly wheel by standing on a spoke until the engine caught. Snow claimed that after a tune-up in the fall of 1908 the pump was so powerful that it sucked all the water out of the irrigation ditch.

> *And Arthur Joseph, why he had a Guernsey heifer out to pasture on the edge of the main crick and she slipped and fell into the stream. The dern pump sucked her right up the irrigation ditch, and if I hadn't been out inspectin' the intake pipe, she'd a-been squeezed right through that centrifugal pump. Talk about suction!*

The Yankees and the Portuguese of Victorian Truro

Summer brought the second-home owners and vacationers, generating part-time jobs in new resorts and boarding houses. Lacking air conditioning, newly wealthy city dwellers wanted to escape the hot cities in summer. They looked for rural, seaside villages for their vacations. Provincetown especially, and Truro to a much lesser extent, were favorite destinations for those who sought a picturesque and remote setting. They often stayed a month or two. A later visitor would write about the "beautiful wild sterility of this section of the Cape." The hills of Truro were a treeless expanse of grazing land; most of the homes and gardens were tucked into valleys and hollows.

Women could find summer jobs as chambermaids, kitchen help and waitresses in the resorts—Highland House, the Ballston Beach Cottage Colony and the Corn Hill Cottages—which attracted several hundred vacationers in the summer (*Truro*, Ch. 17). The men worked in the stables and drove the carriages that carried vacationers from the railroad station and on excursions. Building and expanding the vacation resorts as well as a number of summer cottages for second-home owners provided work for carpenters.

Roads were few and mostly unimproved sand tracks. A common way of traveling was walking over footpaths, cow paths and cart ways that interlaced Truro from end to end. A gazetteer noted in 1874, "There are few carriage roads but many private footpaths leading sometimes over bogs by foot-bridges, from house to house." Maps of the time show a web-like pattern of interlinking, intersecting paths between houses, pastures and villages.

During the 1890s, the town marshaled resources to improve its roads and unexpectedly received a matching grant from a wealthy Wellfleet businessman. The town hired about a half dozen men to work more or less regularly on Truro's roads, smoothing and grading them for the increasing number of wagons and carriages and clearing them of snowdrifts. As the workload increased, the town bought two horse-drawn scrapers and a roller. One year, nearly two dozen men worked part-time for the town on its roads. Another year, 150 men earned a few dollars each shoveling snow from the roads.

A state project to "macadamize" the sand road to Wellfleet also provided jobs for Truro men. By the end of the 1890s, the state had graded and macadamized about half the distance with a hardening mixture of gravel and clay. To complete the work, Captain Lorenzo Dow Baker of Wellfleet, who made a fortune importing bananas and founded the United Fruit Company, offered to donate $1,000 if Truro would appropriate the same amount. Baker had a special interest in the road because he owned a large resort hotel on the harbor in Wellfleet and the Corn Hill Cottages overlooking Cape Cod Bay, in Truro. The town readily approved the deal, Truro's Charlie Snow won the contract to do the grading and the state did the macadamizing. It was called the "State Road" (it's now Old County Road), and eventually the road north was macadamized to the end of Beach Point and the wooden bridge to Provincetown.

About twenty Truro men served in three stations of the U.S. Life-Saving Service on the Atlantic Ocean shore. They spent their time in training exercises, patrolling the beach at night and during storms and rescuing shipwreck survivors (*Truro*, Ch. 15). The deadliest shipwrecks in Truro's history occurred during the 1890s—the wreck of the *Jason* with loss of twenty-four lives and the offshore sinking of the *Portland* in a storm. Both founderings and other shipwrecks littered the Atlantic beach with goods and debris that were salvaged by Truro "mooncussers." Salvaging work and beachcombing were not insignificant employment opportunities.

Truro men found employment as station masters at three of the town's four railroad stations (the fourth being a flag stop), and also as laborers who maintained the tracks, roadbed, bridges and stations. Men were also paid to put out brush fires, sometimes quite extensive, caused by sparks from the locomotive smokestacks.

More than half a dozen men and women ran country stores. During the 1890s, despite the town's decline, there were two in North Truro, three in Truro Center and

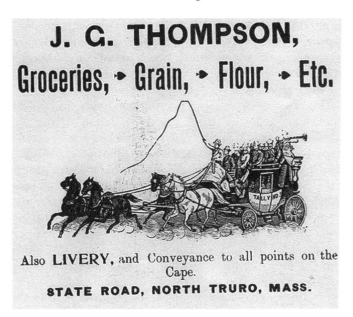

An advertisement from Resident and Business Directory of Cape Cod, 1901.

one in South Truro. A store was often the post office, too, when it was not in someone's front parlor. Lillian J. Small took over her father's grocery store in North Truro, added "dry goods, drugs and fancy articles" and became the postmistress in 1889. Traveling salesmen brought merchandise from manufacturers and the latest gossip from neighboring towns.

Samuel Paine had a general store and pharmacy in Truro Center. He won the town's first liquor license, but he could sell liquors only "for medicinal, chemical and mechanical purposes...at his apothecary store." The license not only prohibited sales "to a person known to be a drunk, and/or to an intoxicated person or to a minor," but ordered that there be "no disorder, indecency, prostitution, lewdness or illegal gambling on the premises." Deyo's history says there were taverns on the main road through Truro, although he notes that no one could recall the names of tavern keepers. Town meetings repeatedly voted overwhelmingly against granting licenses to sell intoxicating liquors, and a special town meeting in 1892 even voted $100 "for the suppression of the liquor traffic."

The country stores sold a variety of tonics and patent medicines, many of them based on opium derivatives, alcohol or both. They no doubt stocked some of the heavily advertised national brands, Fletcher's Castoria, Lydia Pinkham's Vegetable Compound and Doan's Liver Pills. Schelerth says that "whatever affliction troubled the American man, woman or child, patent medicines promised a cure for it." Home remedies continued in use—baking soda for a stomachache, sassafras tea for measles, flaxseed poultices for boils and carbuncles, mullein leaves wrapped around the neck for a sore throat. Quarantine at home limited the spread of measles, whooping cough and scarlet fever among school-age children. As a last resort, a doctor from Provincetown or Wellfleet might make a home call and provide a more or less accurate diagnosis, but there was little else he could do. The most dangerous diseases were still beyond his competence. Medicine had not yet produced a cure for tuberculosis, the most widespread deadly disease, nor for most other contagious diseases. "Despite advances in medical care," says Schlereth, "Victorian America remained an unhealthy and often deadly place. Life expectancy improved if one lived to adulthood, but infancy and childhood remained dangerous life stages." Infant mortality was about 10 percent in the first year of life.

Truro had no undertakers. The deceased's body was prepared for burial by an undertaker elsewhere on the Outer Cape and taken home in a coffin for viewing and prayers. On the burial day, the Portuguese held a funeral service and mass at the Roman Catholic Church. Protestants generally held a prayer service at home. The deceased's trip to the cemetery was in the town-owned hearse, which had its own garage. Marshall says funerals were "most austere." The horse-drawn, black hearse, its

An advertisement for four Truro businesses in 1901.

glass sides draped with a curtain of dark fringe, he says, was a "rather depressing vehicle."

Truro's schools in the 1890s employed seven or eight teachers, all women and all unmarried. (Back in 1871, the town had voted to hire women as teachers instead of men but without giving any explanation.) Two of them were Truro natives, including the revered Betsy Holsbery. The rest came from New England towns and boarded with a family during the school year. There were four schoolhouses for about 150 pupils, and everyone walked to their neighborhood school. The town's spending for books, supplies, maps and blackboards was generous, around $200 a year. In 1898, two of the schools got both an organ and a part-time music teacher. Daylight through the windows was the only lighting, and in winter coal-burning stoves heated the schoolroom. Although well over half the pupils were from Portuguese families, the school board's annual reports do not indicate that the teachers had any difficulty teaching children from Portuguese-speaking families.

When school was not in session, children had chores around the house and farm. Parents still held that children at an early age should become productive members of the family, but this was beginning to change. After the turn of the century, they would recognize childhood and adolescence as separate stages in life, defined by socio-psychological studies and popular culture. Still, in contrast to their grandparents' youth, Truro's children in the 1890s had more fun.

Roller-skating and dancing were the main manifestations of the Gay Nineties in Truro. For a while, Truro had two roller-skating rinks. One was an old school building located near Mill Pond, which was taken apart in 1895, moved to Truro Center and converted into the first Roman Catholic Church. Isaac M. ("Mort") Small had a hundred-foot-long roller rink at his Highland resort. He said that "on holidays the place would be crowded, an orchestra would be engaged and then after a skating session dancing would follow through the night. It was a very enjoyable sport in which old and young could engage." A gale destroyed the building in 1898. In winter, there was skating on ponds and the upper Pamet River, and sledding on snow-packed roads.

People gathered for dances, songfests, lectures and an occasional theatrical on the second floor of Town Hall and in a building called the "Village Hall" in North Truro. The town laid new flooring in Town Hall, bought an organ and paid W.W. Cobb $50 to be the organist. Card parties and box suppers were also held at Town Hall. The country stores and the blacksmith's shop in Truro Center were informal places to meet and trade gossip.

Church services and church socials at Town Hall continued to be centers of courtship for young people. Another occasion to get together was town meeting, which was held two or three times a year. These were day-long events, and the ladies of the Methodist Episcopal Sewing Circle supplied food and drink for the dinner break at midday. Like the rest of America, even in hard times, Truro people were joiners. "Social circles are well attended," says Deyo's history, "Societies and associations...are composed of members from the entire town." One of them was the Truro Library Association, which according to Deyo, held "literary entertainments."

Epilogue

After the turn of the century, everyday life in Truro would be quiet and uneventful for more than fifty years. Yankees continued to leave. Portuguese immigration tapered off. More farm families abandoned their properties. The population decline would not bottom out until 1930, when there were only five hundred residents in Truro—fewer than two hundred households.

Electricity, telephones and automobiles would arrive in the early decades of the 1900s, and homeowners began to install indoor plumbing. Still, with fewer and fewer people living in Truro, it remained a rural, seaside town untouched by development and slower to install modern conveniences than most of New England. When the summer vacation season ended and the visitors returned home, Truro was one of the smallest towns of small-town America. Some might even have called it a backwater.

Everyday life in those years would be chronicled with affection by two Truro writers. In his memoir, Anthony L. Marshall recalled what it was like living in Truro as a boy and teenager in the decade or two before 1920. That was the year Tom Kane arrived in Truro as a youngster. Starting in the 1940s, he wrote newspaper columns for almost five decades about the townsfolk and their everyday life in the time of his youth and adult years. The best of his columns are collected in his book, *My Pamet*.

Agnes Edwards, who visited Truro a few years before 1920, described a "half-desolate and wholly fascinating landscape" in her book, *Cape Cod, New and Old*:

The solitary and distant houses of which we may see only a bit of the roof; with their little gardens lying like bracelets around their bases; with their stunted trees, and low levels of red and brown, wind-licked marshes with their inlets and creeks; and with their churches placed high on an occasional crest, like the little rocky chapels on the Cornish coast of England—this is Truro!

She contrasted the landscape of Truro with that of the rest of Cape Cod:

If you wish to view mile after mile of wild barrens, where the vegetation is chiefly moss, and where the sand after every storm drifts over the heads of the submerged bushes and piles up around decaying fence rails; where there is hardly a boulder as big as your hand, or even gravel, and the layer of soil is so thin that you can kick it off with your toe—then go to Truro.

The town's rural, seaside atmosphere—next door to, but distinct from, the colorful art colony in Provincetown—drew the first artists and writers in the 1920s and 1930s, including John Dos Passos, Edna St. Vincent Millay, Edmund Wilson, Edward Hopper and Ben Shahn. They bought or rented farm houses and cottages in Truro, some for the summer months, some for longer sojourns (*Truro*, Ch. 18).

Those were the days that old-timers now recall with nostalgia—the days before increasing numbers of retirees began buying and building retirement homes and wealthy vacationers began buying and building second homes as close to Cape Cod Bay and the Pamet River as they could afford. The retirees and second-home owners gradually transformed everyday life in Truro from the hard physical labor of farming, fishing and whaling to a life of leisure, recreation, creative endeavors and retirement for the typical homeowner—a twentieth century "immigrant" from off-Cape cities (*Truro*, Ch. 19).

Selected Reading 1
The Indians Observed

Excerpts from "The Second Part" of *New England's Prospect* by William Wood, who was in the Boston area from 1629 to 1634 (see also Martin Pring's narrative in Appendix A in *Truro: The Story of a Cape Cod Town)*:

To enter into a serious discourse concerning the natural conditions of these [southern New England] Indians might procure admiration from the people of any civilized nations, in regard of the civility and good natures.... These Indians are of affable, courteous and well-disposed natures, ready to communicate the best of their wealth to the mutual good of one another; and the less abundance they have to manifest their entire friendship, so much the more perspicuous is their love in that they are as willing to part with their mite in poverty as treasure in plenty....

I have been amongst diverse of them, yet did I never see any falling out amongst them, not so much as cross words or reviling speeches which might provoke to blows....I have known when four of these milder spirits have sat down, staking their treasures, where they have played four and twenty hours, neither eating, drinking or sleeping in the interim; nay, which is most to be wondered at, not quarreling, but as they came thither in peace so they depart in peace. When he that had lost all his wampompeag, his house, his kettle, his beaver, his hatchet, his knife, yea all his little all, having nothing left but his naked self, was as merry as they that won it. So in sports of activity: at football...if any man be thrown, he laughs out his foil. There is no seeking of revenge, no quarreling, no bloody noses, scratched faces, black eyes, broken shins, no bruised members or crushed ribs, the lamentable effects of rage. But the goal being won, the goods on one side lost, friends they were at football and friends they must meet at the kettle....

Now of their worships. As it is natural to all mortals to worship something, so do these people, but exactly to describe to whom their worship is chiefly bent is very difficult. They acknowledge especially two: Ketan, who is their good god, to whom they sacrifice (as the ancient heathen did to Ceres) after their garners be full with a good crop; upon this god likewise they invocate for fair weather, for rain in time of drought, and for the recovery of their sick. But if they do not hear them, their powwows betak[e] themselves to their exorcisms and necromantic charms by which they bring to pass strange things if we may believe the Indians....

The manner of their action in their conjuration is thus: the parties that are sick or lame being brought before them, the powwow sitting down, the rest of the Indians giving attentive audience to his imprecations and invocations, and after the violent expression of many a hideous bellowing and groaning, he makes a stop, and then all the auditors with one voice utter a short canto. Which done, the powwow still proceeds in his invocations, sometimes roaring like a bear, other times groaning like a dying horse, foaming at the mouth like a chased boar, smiting his naked breast and things with such violence as if he were mad. Thus will he continue sometimes half a day, spending his lungs, sweating out his fat and tormenting his body in this diabolical worship....

To speak of their games...spending half their days in gaming and lazing: they have two sorts of games, one called *puim*, the other hubbub, not much unlike cards and dice.... Puim is fifty or sixty small bents [rushes] of a foot long, which they divide to the number of gamesters, shuffling them first between the palms of their hands; he that hath more than his fellow is so much the forwarder in his game. Many other strange whimseys be in this game, which would be too long to commit to paper. He that is a noted gamester had a great hole in his ear wherein he carries his puims in defiance of his antagonists.

Hubbub is five small bones in a small, smooth tray; the bones be like a die but something flatter, black on one side and white on the other, which they place on the ground, against which, violently thumping the platter, the bones mount, changing colors with the windy whisking of their hands to and fro; which action in that sport they much use, smiting themselves on the breast and thighs, crying out "hub, hub, hub, hub." They may be heard play at this game a quarter of a mile off. The bones being all black and white make a double game; if three be of a color and two of another, then they afford but a single game; four of a color and one differing is nothing. So long as a man wins he keeps the tray, but if he lose the next man takes it. They are so bewitched with these two games that they will lose sometimes all they have....

For their sports of activity they have commonly but three or four, as football, shooting, running and swimming. Their goals [for football, i.e. soccer] be a mile long, placed in the sands, which are as even as a board. Their ball is no bigger than a handball, which sometimes they mount in the air with their naked feet; sometimes it is swayed by the multitude; sometimes also it is two days before they get a goal. Then they mark the ground they win and begin there the next day....

For their shooting they be most desperate marksmen for a point blank object....Such is their celerity and dexterity in artillery that they can smite the swift-running hind and nimble-winked pigeon without a standing pause or left-eyed blinking. They draw their arrows between the forefingers and the thumb. Their bows be quick but not very strong.... These men shoot at one another, but with swift conveyance shun the arrow. This they do to make themselves expert against time of war. It hath often been admired how they can find their arrows, be the weeds as high as themselves, yet they take such perfect notice of the flight and fall that they seldom lose any. They are trained up to their bows even from their childhood; little boys with bows made of little sticks and arrows of great bents [rushes] will smite down a piece of tobacco pipe every shoot a good way off. As these Indians be good marksmen, so are they well experienced where the very life of every creature lieth and know where to smite him to make him die presently.

For their swimming, it is almost natural, but much perfected by continual practice. Their swimming is not after our English fashion of spread arms and legs, which they hold too tiresome, but like dogs their arms before them cutting through the liquids with their right shoulder. In this manner, they swim very swift and far, either in rough or smooth waters, sometimes for their ease lying as still as a log. Sometimes they will play the dive-doppers and come up in unexpected places. Their children likewise be taught to swim when they are very young.

For their running, it is with much celerity and continuance, yet I suppose there be many Englishmen who, being as lightly clad as they are, would outrun them for a spurt, though not be able to continue it for a day or days, being they [the Indians] be very strong-winded and rightly clad for a race.

For their hunting...having certain hunting houses in such places where they know the deer usually doth frequent, in which they keep themselves rendezvous, their snares, and all their accouterments for that employment. When they get sight of a deer, moose or bear, they study how to get the [up]wind of him, and approaching within shot, stab their mark quite through, if the bones hinder not....They hunt likewise after wolves and wildcats, raccoons, otters, beavers, musquashes, trading both their skins and flesh to the English.

Besides their artillery, they have other devices to kill their game, as sometimes hedges a mile or two miles long, being a mile wide at one end and made narrower and narrower by degrees, leaving only a gap of six feet long over against which, in the daytime, they lie lurking to shoot the deer which come through that narrow gut....In the night, at the gut of this hedge they set deer traps, which are springs made of young trees and smooth-wrought cords, so strong as it will toss a horse if he be caught in it....

Of their fishing, in this trade they be very expert, being experienced in the knowledge of all baits, fitting sundry baits for several fishes and diverse seasons; being not ignorant likewise of the removal of fishes, knowing when to fish rivers and when at rocks, when in bays, and when at seas. [They make lines] of their own hemp more curiously wrought of stronger materials than ours, hooked with bone hooks....They make likewise very strong sturgeon nets with which they catch sturgeons twelve, fourteen and sixteen, some eighteen foot long, in the daytime. In the nighttime, they betake them to their birchen canoes, in which they carry a forty-fathom line with a sharp, bearded dart fastened at the end thereof. Then lighting a blazing torch made of birchen rods, they weave it to and again by their canoe side, which the sturgeon, much delighted with, come to them tumbling and playing, turning up his white belly, into which they thrust their lance, his back being impenetrable. Which done, they haul to the shore their struggling prize. they have often recourse unto the rocks whereupon the sea beats, in warm weather, to look out for sleepy seals, whose oil they much esteem, using it for diverse things. In summer, they seldom fish anywhere but in salt; in winter, in the fresh water and ponds....

Their cordage is so even, soft and smooth that it looks more like silk than hemp. Their sturgeon nets be not deep, nor above thirty or forty foot long, which in ebbing low waters they stake fast to the ground where they are sure the sturgeon will come, never looking more at it till the next low water. Their canoes be made either of pine trees, which... they burned hollow, scraping them smooth with clam shells and oyster shells, cutting their outsides with stone hatchets. These boats be not above a foot and a half or two feet wide and twenty feet long. Their other canoes be made of thin birch rinds, close ribbed on the inside with broad, thin hoops like the hoops of a tub. These are made very light. A man may carry one of them a mile, being made purposely to carry from river to river and bay to bay, to shorten land passages. In these cockling fly-boats, wherein an Englishman can scarce sit without a fearful tottering, they will venture to sea when an English shallop dare not bear a knot of sail, scudding over the overgrown waves as fast as a wind-driven ship, being driven by their paddles.... If a cross wave (as is seldom) turn her keel upside down, they by swimming free her and scramble into her again....

Of their women...their persons and features being every way correspondent [*sic*], their qualifications more excellent, being more loving, pitiful and modest, mild, provident and laborious than their lazy husbands.

Their employments be many: first, their building of houses, whose frames are formed like our garden arbors, sometimes more round, very strong and handsome, covered with close-wrought mats of their own weaving, which deny entrance to any drop of rain, though it come both fierce and long, neither can the piercing north wind find a cranny through which he can convey his cooling breath. They be warmer than our English houses. At the top is a square hole for the smoke's evacuation, which in rainy weather is covered with a [mat]. These be such smoky dwellings that when there is good fires they are not able to stand upright, but lie all along under the smoke, never using any stools or chairs....When their families be dispersed by reason of heat and occasions...[the women] are often troubled like snails to carry their houses on their backs, sometimes to fishing places, other times to hunting places, after that to a planting place where it abides the longest.

Another work is their planting of corn, wherein they exceed our English husbandmen, keeping it so clear with their clamshell hoes as if it were a garden rather than a corn field, not suffering a choking weed to advance his audacious head above their infant corn or an undermining worm to spoil his spurns. Their corn being ripe, they gather it, and drying it hard in the sun, convey it to their barns, which be great holes digged in the ground in form of a brass pot, sealed with rinds of trees, wherein they put their corn....

Another of their employments is their summer processions to get lobsters for their husbands, wherewith they bait their hooks when they go afishing for bass or codfish. This is an everyday's walk, be the weather cold or hot, the waters rough or calm. They must dive sometimes over head and ears for a lobster, which often shakes them by their hands with a churlish nip and bids them *adieu*. The tide being spent, they trudge home two or three miles with a hundredweight of lobsters at their backs, and if none, a hundred scowls meet them at home and a hungry belly for two days after. Their husbands having caught any fish, they bring it in their boats as far as they can by water and there leave it; as it was their care to catch it, so it must be the wives' pains to fetch it home, or fast. Which done, they must dress it and cook it, dish it, and present it....In the summer, these Indian women, when lobsters be in their plenty and prime, they dry them to keep for winter, erecting scaffolds in the hot sunshine, making fires likewise underneath them (by whose smoke the flies are expelled) till the substance remain hard and dry. In this manner, they dry bass and other fishes without salt, cutting them very thin to dry suddenly before the flies spoil them or the rain moist them, having a special care to hang them in their smoky houses in the night and dankish weather.

In summer, they gather flags [cattails], of which they make mats for houses, and hemp and rushes, with dyeing stuff, of which they make curious baskets with intermixed colors and protractures of antic imagery. These baskets be of all sizes....In winter, they are their husbands caterers, trudging to the clam banks for their belly timber and their porters to lug home their venison, which their laziness exposes to the wolves till they impose it upon their wives' shoulders. They likewise sew their husbands' shoes and weave coats of turkey feathers, besides all their ordinary household drudgery, which daily lies upon them, so that a big belly hinders no business, nor a childbirth takes much time, but the young infant being greased and sooted [dyed?], wrapped in a beaver skin, bound to his good behavior with his feet up to his bum upon a board two foot long and one foot broad, his face exposed to all nipping weather, this little papoose travels about with his bare-footed mother to paddle in the icy clam banks after three or four days of age have sealed his passboard and his mother's recovery.

For their carriage, it is very civil, smiles being the greatest grace of their mirth; their music is lullabies to quiet their children, who generally are as quiet as if they had neither spleen or lungs. To hear one of these Indians unseen, a good ear might easily mistake their untaught voice for the warbling of a well-tuned instrument, such command have they of their voices.

These women's modesty drives them to wear more clothes than their men, having always a coat of cloth of skins wrapped like a blanket about their loins, reaching down to their hams, which they never put off in company....

Although the Indians be of lusty [vigorous] and healthful bodies, not experimentally knowing the catalogue of those health-wasting diseases which are incident to other countries, as fevers, pleurisies, callentures, agues, obstructions, consumptions, subfumigations, convulsions, apoplexies, dropsies, gouts, stones, toothaches, pox, measles, or the like, but spin out the thread of their days to a fair length, numbering threescore, fourscore, some a hundred years, before the world's universal summoner cite them to the craving grave.

But the date of their life expired, and death's arrestment seizing upon them, all hope of recovery being past, then to behold and hear their throbbing sobs and deep-fetched sighs, their grief-wrung hands and tear-bedewed cheeks, their doleful cries, would draw tears from adamantine eyes that be but spectators of their mournful obsequies. The glut of their grief being past, they commit the corpses of their deceased friends to the ground, over whose grave is for a long time spent many a briny tear, deep groan, and Irish-like howlings, continuing annual mournings with a black, stiff paint on their faces. These are the mourners without hope, yet do they hold the immortality of the never-dying soul that it shall pass to the southwest Elysium....

Selected Reading 2

A Settler's Will

Thomas Paine (1657–1721), one of the earliest settlers of Pamet in the 1680s, died the richest man in Truro. His will and inventory provide a glimpse into his life and concerns, even though he was not a typical settler and four decades had passed since he arrived. These excerpts silently modernize and regularize the language of the will:

In the name of God amen the sixth day of April, Anno Domini 1720, in the sixth year of the reign of our Sovereign Lord, George, King of Great Britain I, Thomas Paine of Truro in the County of Barnstable in the Province of Massachusetts Bay, being of perfect mind and memory, thanks be given to God, being not unmindful of the mortality of my body, and knowing that it is appointed for all men once to die, do make and ordain this my last will and testament.

I give and bequeath to Elizabeth, my beloved wife, the use and improvement of [income or gain from] all the new parts of my dwelling house wherein I now live and the improvement of one half of the farm, that is, the upland and meadow lying about my house on the northern side of the meadow with the one half of all my meadows lying near my house between Indian Neck [Tom's Hill] and my other land and the benefit of one half of my barn.

Furthermore, I will and bequeath to my wife, Elizabeth, one third part of my personal estate, goods and chattels (after my just debts and funeral charges are paid and discharged) to have and enjoy to her and her assigns forever.

[Here follows eight paragraphs dividing his extensive land holdings among his six sons.]

I give and bequeath to my son Thomas Paine my two Negroes [Gaston?] and [Molly?] but inasmuch as my said two Negroes are now grown in years and more likely to be a charge than is proper to him or to any that shall take charge of them, I do therefore give unto my son Thomas Paine, his heirs and assigns my windmill with all the appurtenances to her belonging and that parcel whereon she standeth... provided my said son will accept of my said Negroes on these conditions and will fulfill my engagements to the Town referring to the windmill; but if my said son Thomas will not accept of my said Negroes on said conditions, then my son Joshua shall have the liberty if he shall see cause to take them on the same conditions, but if he also shall refuse them, any other of my sons shall have liberty to take them on said conditions.

I give unto my son Thomas Paine my blue suit of wearing apparel, my pistols, rapier...[for] all the rest of my wearing apparel, my will is that they shall be equally divided among my five sons aforenamed.

I give unto my sons Joshua Paine and Barnabas Paine all my [black]smith's tools.

I give and bequeath unto my daughter Phebe Paine forty pounds to be paid her by my executors out of my personal estate; and all the residue and [remains?] of my personal estate, goods and chattels I give and bequeath to my four daughters, [Hannah Paine?], Abigail White, Phebe Paine and Lidia Hinckley, to be equally divided among them.

I give to my said four daughters to have and to hold to them and their heirs and assigns forever my two lots of land lying on the southerly side of Pamets Great River, and the line between Eastham and Truro being the ninth lot in the eastern division [of his lands] and the eighth lot in the westerly division of said lands, to be sold by them in equal right..

The inventory taken by us subscribers of all the estate of the honorable Thomas Paine Esq., late deceased in Truro [selected personal items]:

The gentleman's wearing apparel, woolen and linen, silver and leather, all wigs and snuff:
28 pounds 14 shillings.
In the parlor, one bed and bedstead and all furniture [bedding] belonging to them: 11 pounds 16 shillings.
Three beds and bedsteads and all furniture: 29 pounds 16 shillings.
Six pair of pillow cases, nine pair of sheets: 9 pounds 1 shilling.
Window curtains and rods: 17 shillings.
Clock and watch, looking glass and pictures: 10 pounds 10 shillings.
All pots, kettles and household iron ware: 12 pounds.
Pewter and tin [dishes and utensils], grindstone: 7 pounds 6 shillings.
Sheep's wool with two spinning wheels: 4 pounds 14 shillings.
Three guns, wedges, axes: 3 pounds 11 shillings.
Books and letters: 10 pounds 6 shillings.
Carpenter and cooper's tools: 3 pounds 16 shillings.
The land measuring chain, scales and weights: 1 pound 5 shillings.
Apothecary stuff: 3 pounds 3 shillings.
Tobacco: 4 shillings.

Selected Reading 3

Advice for the Housewife of the Early 1800s

Excerpts from *The American Frugal Housewife* by Mrs. Lydia Maria Child (1802–1880), from the 12th edition (1832), reflecting aspects of the life of a Truro fisherman's wife:

The writer has no apology to offer for this cheap little book of economical hints, except her deep conviction that such a book is needed....Books of this kind have usually been written for the wealthy; I have written for the poor....I have attempted to teach how money can be *saved*, not how it can be enjoyed.

ODD SCRAPS FOR THE ECONOMICAL

If you would avoid waste in your family, attend to the following rules, and do not despise them because they appear so unimportant.

Look frequently to the pails, to see that nothing is thrown to the pigs which should have been in the grease pot.

Look to the grease pot, and see that nothing is there which might have served to nourish your own family, or a poorer one.

See that the beef and pork are always *under* the brine and that the brine is sweet and clean.

Count towels, sheets, spoons, etc., occasionally, that those who use them may not become careless.

See that the vegetables are neither sprouting nor decaying. If they are so, remove them to a drier place and spread them.

Examine preserves to see that they are not contracting mold, and your pickles to see that they are not growing soft and tasteless.

Indian meal and rye meal are in danger of fermenting in summer, particularly Indian. They should be kept in a cool place and stirred open to the air once in a while. A large stone put in the middle of a barrel of meal, is a good thing to keep it cool.

Spirits of turpentine is good to take grease spots out of woolen clothes, to take spots of paint, etc., from mahogany furniture, and to cleanse white kid gloves. Cockroaches and all vermin have an aversion to spirits of turpentine.

An ounce of quicksilver beat up with the white of two eggs and put on with a feather is the cleanest and surest bed-bug poison. What is left should be thrown away; it is dangerous to have about the house. If the vermin are in your walls, fill up the cracks with *verdigris*-green paint.

Lamps will have a less disagreeable smell if you dip your wick-yarn in strong, hot vinegar and dry it.

Those who make candles will find it a great improvement to steep the wicks in lime water and saltpeter and dry them. The flame is clearer and the tallow will not "run."

Eggs will keep almost any length of time in lime water properly prepared. One pint of coarse salt and one pint of unslaked lime to a pail of water. If there be too much lime, it will eat the shells from the eggs; and if there be a single egg cracked, it will spoil the whole. They should be covered with lime water and kept in a cold place. The yolk becomes slightly red, but I have seen eggs, thus kept, perfectly sweet and fresh at the end of three years....

Barley straw is best for beds; dry corn husks, slit into shreds, are far better than straw.

Straw beds are much better for being boxed at the sides in the same manner upholsterers prepare ticks for feathers....

In winter, always set the handle of your pump as high as possible before you go to bed. Except in very frigid weather, this keeps the handle from freezing. When there is reason to apprehend extreme cold, do not forget to throw a rug or horse blanket over your pump; a frozen pump is comfortless preparation for a winter's breakfast....

It is thought to be a preventive to the unhealthy influence of cucumbers to cut the slices very thin and drop each one into cold water as you cut it. A few minutes in the water takes out a large portion of the slimy matter, so injurious to health. They should be eaten with high seasoning....

Poke root boiled in water and mixed with a good quantity of molasses, set about the kitchen, the pantry, etc. in large deep plates, will kill cockroaches in great numbers and finally rid the house of them. The Indians say that poke root boiled into a soft poultice is the cure for the bite of a snake. I have heard of a fine horse saved by it.

SIMPLE REMEDIES

Cotton wool, wet with sweet oil and paregoric, relieves the ear ache very soon.

A good quantity of old cheese is the best thing to eat when distressed by eating too much fruit, or oppressed with any kind of food. Physicians have given it in cases of extreme danger.

Honey and milk is very good for worms; so is strong salt water; likewise powdered sage and molasses taken freely.

For a sudden attack of quincy or croup, bathe the neck in bear's grease and pour it down the throat. A linen rag soaked in sweet oil, butter or lard and sprinkled with yellow Scotch snuff is said to have performed wonderful cures in cases of croup; it should be placed where the distress is greatest. Goose grease or any kind of oily grease is as good as bear's oil.

Equal parts of camphor, spirits of wine and hartshorn, well mixed and rubbed upon the throat, is said to be good for the croup.

A poultice of wheat bran or rye bran and vinegar very soon takes down the inflammation occasioned by a sprain.

Brown paper, wet, is healing to a bruise. Dipped in molasses, it is said to take down inflammation.

If you happen to cut yourself slightly while cooking, bind on some fine salt; molasses is likewise good.

Flour boiled thoroughly in milk so as to make quite a thick porridge is good in cases of dysentery. A tablespoon of W.I. rum, a tablespoon of sugar-baker's molasses and the same quantity of sweet oil, well simmered together, is likewise good for this disorder; the oil softens the harshness of the other ingredients.

Black or green tea, steeped in boiling milk, seasoned with nutmeg and sugar is excellent for the dysentery. Cork burnt to charcoal, about as big as a hazelnut, macerated and put in a teaspoonful of brandy, with a little loaf of sugar and nutmeg, is very efficacious in cases of dysentery and cholera-morbus. If nutmeg be wanting, peppermint water may be used. Flannel wet with brandy, powdered with Cayenne pepper, and laid upon the bowels affords great relief in cases of extreme distress....

Blackberries are extremely useful in cases of dysentery. To eat the berries is very healthy; tea made of the roots and leaves is beneficial; and a syrup made of the berries is still better. Blackberries have sometimes effected a cure when physicians despaired.

A stocking bound on warm from the foot, at night, is good for the sore throat.

An ointment made from the common ground worms, which boys dig to bait fishes, rubbed on with the hand, is said to be excellent, when the sinews are drawn up by any disease or accident....

If a wound bleeds very fast, and there is no physician at hand, cover it with the scrapings of sole leather, scraped like coarse lint. This stops blood very soon....

Tea made of slippery elm is good for the piles and for humors in the blood, to be drank plentifully. Winter evergreen* is considered good for all humors, particularly scrofula. Some call it rheumatism weed because a tea made from it is supposed to check that painful disorder. (*This plant resembles the poisonous kill-lamb both in shape and the glossiness of the leaves. Great care should be taken to distinguish them.)

An ointment of lard, sulphur and cream of tartar, simmered together, is good for the piles....

The constant use of malt beer, or malt in any way, is said to be a preservative against fevers.

Black-cherry tree bark, barberry bark, mustard seed, petty morel root and horseradish, well steeped in cider, are excellent for the jaundice.

A poultice made of ginger or of common chickweed that grows about one's door in the country has given great relief to the tooth ache, when applied frequently to the cheek.

A spoonful of ashes stirred in cider is good to prevent sickness of the stomach. Physicians frequently order it in cases of cholera-morbus....

Boil castor oil with an equal quantity of milk, sweeten it with a little sugar, stir it well, and, when cold, give it to children for drink. They will never suspect it is medicine and will even love the taste of it.

Cotton wool and oil are the best things for a burn. When children are burned, it is difficult to make them endure the application of cotton wool. I have known the inflammation of a very bad burn extracted in one night by the constant application of brandy, vinegar and water mixed together. This feels cool and pleasant, and a few drops of paregoric will soon put the little sufferer to sleep.

Selected Readings 4

The Portuguese and the Yankees

Excerpts from the economic and demographic study of Cape Cod published by the Commonwealth of Massachusetts in 1897:

Truro differs much from Provincetown, as it has neither harbor nor fishing vessels. Instead, we find a long bay with shallow water, well adapted to fish weirs or traps, which completely line the shore, supplying fish for the market, and furnishing bait for the fishing vessels of Boston, Gloucester, Provincetown and other places. This for a number of years has been a paying industry, but during the last year or two results have been poor. Formerly this town had a small tide harbor at the mouth of the Pamet River, where quite a fleet of small mackerel fishing vessels was built and owned. These were for a long time successful, but when the harbor became filled with sand, as such harbors usually do, they went to other places where harbors were better adapted to the business. Finally, when the mackerel fisheries failed, the fishermen turned their attention to fish weirs or traps. It is a new method of taking fish in this section and does not occupy all the time of the men. Most of them cultivate gardens and find a ready market for their produce in the neighboring towns. The Western Islanders [Portuguese immigrants from the Azores and Cape Verde islands] form a large part of the crews engaged on these weirs. The women are very industrious out of doors as well as in.

The large fresh-water pond near the Highlands or High Head of Truro, called East Harbor, was enclosed with a dike by the state in 1869. This dike is crossed by the railroad near Provincetown. The year before, 1868, the national government placed a dike at the upper end of this pond to protect the harbor of Provincetown from the encroachments of the ocean on the outer beach, as it had broken through several times. This dike had a sluiceway to drain off the water from the upper meadow. The lower, or state dike, is a closed one, and since it was built it has operated to collect sand on the bayside, until there is now a wide beach. The average depth of this pond is about six feet. The water in the pond comes from these Highlands [i.e. High Head], as they form a perfect watershed, being composed largely of clay and heavy loam. There are springs running out from [it], seen mostly in the summer when the pond is low....There are fine farms, under a good state of cultivation. The large pond of fresh water near them might be utilized in irrigation. Irrigation has never been tried in Truro. The land...is owned and cultivated by natives, the Western Islanders having never settled there.

Different opinions are expressed as to the effect of the closed dike upon the meadow above. Some think it has been detrimental, causing the loss of the salt hay which was utilized for cattle, the marsh now being overrun with flags [cattails] and other wild growths. Others think the fresh meadow has been of some value. It requires considerable labor to maintain the dike. Along the edges there are some wet gardens.

At North Truro what was once a large pond or swamp has been filled in quite extensively from time to time. It has proved a good meadow and maintains vegetable gardens in dry season. Part of this was made into cranberry bogs with fair success. This village seems prosperous and is the headquarters of a number of fish weirs, with a cold storage plant for freezing fresh fish and a fish canning factory. The residents are largely interested in farming as well as fishing. For a number of years after these fish weirs were established they were very successful; for the past two or three years the contrary is true. Whether this means that the fish weirs are destroying the fisheries remains to be seen; but the question is troubling the fishermen of the Cape exceedingly. To put a stop to this mode of fishing, however, means interference with the employment of a large number of fishermen. The other parts of the town are more or less engaged in the same kind of fishing.

The village [*sic*] situated between North Truro and Long Nook is largely settled by Western Islanders. They have very comfortable homes and are said to keep them in better repair than the former residents. They are mostly engaged in fishing and farming. They show an aptitude for certain branches of agriculture. They are not all confined to this village but have settled in all parts of the town. Wherever they find a cheap place for sale they buy it, and the women being industrious largely assist in the general support of the family. It does not appear that the newcomers compete with the old residents in the way of wages, but it is plain that they can live on a lower income and will thrive where a native would not be contented. It is evident that the native-born young men have gone to the larger towns, leaving their fathers' places vacant.

In investigations upon the Pamet River, it was found that the dike was built in 1869 by the town of Truro for a highway, in place of the old wooden bridge. Its effect upon the salt meadow is said to be unfavorable, as this meadow is now overrun with flags. The river banks, however, and some of the upper meadows have been made into fine gardens, which even in dry seasons do well. Some of the marsh has been turned into cranberry bogs, but they were not a success. On the south bank of this river above the dike the soil is considered good, and most of these places are occupied by the Western Islanders. In the southern part of the town, much the same conditions obtain as elsewhere, a large part of the inhabitants being aged, and as they pass away their places are taken by newcomers.

An excerpt from *Nooks and Crannies of the New England Coast* (1875), wherein the author, Samuel Adams Drake, meets a group of Portuguese women:

There is quite a colony of Portuguese in Provincetown [and in Truro]. In my rambles I met with a band of them returning from the swamp region back of the town. They looked gypsy-like with their swarthy faces and gleaming eyes. The younger women had clear olive complexions, black eyes and the elongated Madonna faces of their race; the older ones were grisly and witch-like, with shriveled bodies and wrinkled faces. All of them bore bundles of fagots on their heads that our tender women would have sunk under, yet they passed by me, and I watched them until out of sight; for picturesque objects anywhere, here they were doubly so. They had all gaudy handkerchiefs tied about their heads and shawls worn sash-wise and knotted at the hip, the bright bits of warm color contrasting kindly with the dead white of the sand. There were shapely figures among them, but the men's boots they of necessity wore subtracted a little from the symmetry of outline and my admiration.

They number about fifty families—these Portuguese— and are increasing. One citizen expressed a vague apprehension lest they should exclude, eventually, the whites, as the whites had expelled the Indians. And why not? They believe in large families, while we believe in small ones or none at all.

A listing of the businesses in Victorian Truro, mostly owned by Yankees, from the *Resident and Business Directory of Cape Cod, Massachusetts, 1901*:

TRURO BUSINESS DIRECTORY

Boarding Houses
Corlew, B.E. (Summer), Castle rd, n. the shore
Hart, W.H. (Summer), off State road, n. Railroad av., N.T.

Carpenter and Builder
Snow, Charles W., Castle road

Clergymen
Bushnell, John J., Rev. (Union), Hillside ave., N.T.
Gunn, Louis G., Rev. (Methodist), Castle road
Thompson, George O., Rev. (Congregational), Main

Coal and Wood
Rich, M.A., and J.L., State road. cor. Highland ave., N.T.

Cold Storage
No. Truro Cold Storage Co., n. the depot, N.T.

Confectionery, etc.
(See also Grocers)
Grozier, Betsey S., Main, cor. State road, N.T.
Small, Elizabeth F., Mrs., State road, n. Main, N.T.

Dry Goods and Fancy Goods
Grozier, Betsey S., Main, cor. State road, N.T.
Small, Elizabeth F., Mrs., State road, n. Main, N.T.
Snow, Mary J., Mrs., P.O. Building

Express
New York and Boston Dispatch

Fish Canning Establishment
Underwood, William Co., n. the depot, N.T.

Fish Dealers
Blackford, J.W., Proprietors Road
Rogers, John, Main

Grocers
Elliott, John, So. Truro at the depot, S.T.
Hart, Burton S., State road, n. Railroad av. N.T.
Paine, Eben F., State road, cor. Castle
Rose, Frank, Castle road, n. the shore
Thompson, J.G., State road, N.T.
Whitman, C.W., State road, cor. Castle

Hairdresser
Nickerson Smith, State road, N.T.

Hay and Grain
Rich, M.A. and J.L., State road cor. Highland ave., N.T.
Ryder, Thomas F., Main, cor. Proprietors road
Thompson, J.G., State road, N.T.

High Breed Cattle
Marshall, A.S., Main

Hotels
Ballston Beach Inn, S.W. Ball, prop.
Central House, E.R. Hopkins, prop. P.O. sq.
Highland House, W.M. Small, prop., Highland ave., N.T.

Justice of the Peace
Dyer, John B., Palmet

Livery Stables
Hopkins, Ezra R., P.O. square.
Small, W.M., Highland, N.T.
Thompson, J.G., State road, N.T.

Milkmen
Cabral, Joseph, State road, n. Railroad ave., N.T.
Marshall, A.S., Main
Rich, M.A., State road, cor. Highland av., N.T.
Small, Edward L., Highland av., N.T.
Sparrow, J.A., Main, N.T.
Williams, F.K., Long Nook Hollow

Music Teacher
Gardner, Henrietta P., Castle road

Nurse
Swift, Charles H., Mrs., Higgins hollow

Physician and Surgeon
Connor, Charles B., State road opp. town library

Poultry, etc.
Gould, Benjamin F., South Truro, S.T.
Hatch, Naylor, Main
Holway, Arthur H., State road.

Provisions
Paine, Daniel E., Long Nook hollow

Pumps, Windmills, etc.
Snow, Charles W., Castle road

Real estate
Snow, Isaac, Castle road, n. the shore

Teaming and Jobbing
Hopkins, Ezra R., P.O. square.
Snow, Edwin L., P.O. square

A Chronology of Truro's History

Prehistoric times
13,000 years ago—Ice Age ends, Cape Cod formed
4,000-8,000 years ago—First signs of Indians in Truro
3,000-4,000 years ago—Land north of High Head begins to form
Up to 4,000 years ago—Indian settlements in Truro

The 17th Century
1603—Martin Pring at Pamet Harbor
1620—Pilgrims in Truro for five days
1650s—Pamet Proprietors granted land now Truro
1670—Thomas Paine becomes a majority Pamet Proprietor
1680s—Settlement of Pamet by Paine and others

The 18th Century
1700—Pamet settlers decide to seek a minister
1704—First Congregational meetinghouse built
1709—Pamet made a town called Truro, with forty families
1710—John Avery called to be first minister
1716—First schoolmaster hired
1721—Death of Thomas Paine, Truro's founder
—Congregational meetinghouse rebuilt
1720s—Truro captain among the first American deep-sea whalers
1754—Death of the Reverend John Avery

1757—Truro joins Provincetown to defend against the French
1774—Truro deep-sea whalers at peak of success
—Town meeting supports aims of the Boston Revolutionaries
1775—Town is fired upon by British
1778—British warship Somerset is wrecked; prisoners taken
1794—Freeman publishes first description of Truro
—Methodist meetinghouse built
1797—The first Highland Light is erected

The 19th Century
1812—British cannonballs land in Truro in War of 1812
1827—Congregational meetinghouse built on Town Hall Hill
1830–1855—Fishing, ship-building boom at Pamet Harbor
1831—Second lighthouse built at Highland
1841—Truro loses 57 men and 7 vessels in the October gale
1849—Lighthouse built at Pamet Harbor
1849–1857—Thoreau's four walks in Truro
1852—The Josepha is wrecked, with the loss of 18 lives
1857—Third lighthouse built at Highland
1869—Dike dams East Harbor inlet
1872—Life-saving stations built at Head of Pamet, Highland
1873—The railroad arrives at Truro and Provincetown
1870s—Weir fishing launched
1893—The *Jason* is wrecked, with the loss of 24 lives
—Cold storage plant built to process fish

The 20th Century
1907—Mort Small expands resort with new Highland House
1912—Cobb Memorial Library built
1927— "Jenny Lind Tower" moved to Truro
1935—Truro Central School is built

A Chronology of Truro's History

1938—Hurricane causes great damage
1948—North Truro Air Force Station begins operations
1951—MITRE radar site established in South Truro
1960—Railroad service ends
1961—Cape Cod National Seashore established
1991—New school built
1992—Town charter adopted
1993—New Police/Fire Station built
1996—Highland Light is moved back from the cliff edge
1999—New public library built

Sources

CHAPTER I: THE PAMET INDIANS, AN IDYLLIC LIFE
ABRUPTLY ENDED

[Bradford, William, and Edward Winslow.] *Mourt's Relation*. London:
John Bellamie, 1622. Includes the Pilgrims' discoveries about the
Indians in Truro in 1620 and Winslow's description of the Indians
at Plymouth.

Bragdon, Kathleen J. *Native People of Southern New England, 1500–1650*.
Norman OK: University of Oklahoma Press, 1996. An ethnography
based on a wide range of research studies.

Champlain, Samuel. *The Voyages of Samuel Champlain 1604–1618*. Ed.
W. L. Grant. New York: Barnes and Noble, Inc., 1907. Champlain
describes at some length the Indians he met in the Chatham area.

Dunford, Fred, and Greg O'Brien. *Secrets in the Sand: The Archaeology of
Cape Cod*. Hyannis MA: Parnassus Imprints, 1997.

Gookin, Daniel. *Historical Collections of the Indians in New England*. Boston:
Belknap and Hall, 1792. His account, completed in 1674, includes a
report by a Christian teacher in the mid–1600s who counted seventy-
two church-going Indian adults and teenagers still living in Wellfleet,
Truro and Provincetown, the primary basis for estimating the number
of Indians in Truro.

Hallett, Leaman F. "Cultural Traits of the Southern New England
Indians." In *Massachusetts Historical Society Bulletin*, vol. 15. no. 4
(1954).
———. "Indian Games." vol. 16, no. 2 (1955).

SOURCES

————. "Medicine and Pharmacy of the New England Indians." vol. 17, no. 3. (1956).

Moffett, Ross. "The Hillside Site in Truro, Massachusetts." In *The Bulletin of the Massachusetts Archaeological Society* 11 (November 1949).
————. "Two Indian Sites Near Cornhill, Cape Cod." In *The Bulletin of the Massachusetts Archaeological Society* 4 (1953).
————. "An Unusual Indian Harpoon from Truro." In *The Bulletin of the Massachusetts Archaeological Society* 30 (1969).

Mourt's Relation. See Bradford and Winslow.

Pring (e), Martin. "A Voyage Set Out from the Citie of Bristoll...Under the Command of Me Martin Pringe." In *Purchas His Pilgrims*. Vol. 4. London: Stansby/Fetherstone, 1625. See Quinn and Quinn for an annotated edition.

Quinn, David B. and Alison M. Quinn, eds. *The English New England Voyages 1602–1608*. London: The Hakluyt Society, 1983. Includes an annotated edition of Pring's narrative and extensive commentary and background.

Russell, Howard S. *Indian New England Before the Mayflower*. Hanover NH: University Press of New England, 1980. An excellent survey of the way Indians lived in New England.

Salisbury, Neal. *Manitou and Providence: Indians, Europeans, and the Making of New England, 1500–1643*. New York: Oxford University Press, 1982.

Travers, Milton A. *The Wampanoag Indian Federation of the Algonquin Nation: Indian Neighbors of the Pilgrims*. Boston: Christopher House, 1957 and 1961.

Weinstein-Farson, Laurie. *The Wampanoag*. New York: Chelsea House, 1989.

Wilbur, C. Keith. *The New England Indians: An Illustrated Source Book of Authentic Details of Everyday Indian Life*. Old Saybrook CT: The Globe Pequoit Press, 1978. 2nd edition 1996. Rich in illustrations of Indian life and hundred of artifacts.

Wood, William. *New England's Prospect*. London, 1634. 2nd edition, 1635 (at the Houghton Rare Books Library, Harvard University). Reprint, edited, with an introduction by Alden T. Vaughn. Amherst MA: University of Massachusetts Press, 1977. The first book with extensive and generally reliable information on the Indians of New England. Although not the only explorers to describe them, Pring, Winslow and Wood provide the best of the earliest descriptions of the Indians in Truro in the early 1600s, around Plymouth in the early 1620s and in New England in the early 1630s. Wood was based in the Boston area from about 1630 to 1634, just a decade after the Pilgrims arrived.

CHAPTER 2: THE ENGLISH SETTLERS CARVE A LIVING FROM SOIL AND SEA

Axtell, James. *The European and the Indian: Essays in the Ethnohistory of Colonial North America*. New York: Oxford University Press, 1981.

Bailey, R. B. "Pilgrim Possessions" in *They Knew They Were Pilgrims*. Ed. L.D. Gelner. New York: Poseidon, 1971.

Deetz, James J. F. in *Small Things Forgotten: The Archaeology of Early American Life*. Garden City NY: Anchor Press/Doubleday, 1977.

Demos, John. *A Little Commonwealth: Family Life in Plymouth Colony*. New York: Oxford University Press, 1970. See pp 182-5.

Dow, George Francis. *Every Day Life in the Massachusetts Bay Colony*. Boston: Society for the Preservation of New England Antiquities, 1935. Reprint. New York: Dover Publications, 1988.

Earle, Alice Morse. *Home Life in Colonial Days*. New York: Grosset & Dunlap, 1898. Reprint. Berkshire Traveler Press, 1974.

Hawke, David Freeman. *Everyday Life in Early America*. New York: Harper & Row, 1988. An excellent survey.

Kupperman, Karen Ordahl. "Climate and Mastery of the Wilderness in Seventeenth-Century New England" in *Seventeenth-Century New England*. Boston: The Colonial Society of Massachusetts, 1984.

Paine family genealogy, c.1924.

Paine, Thomas. His will, dated April 6, 1720, at the Barnstable MA County Probate Court.

Pamet Proprietor records.

Schweid, Richard. *Consider the Eel*. Chapel Hill and London: University of North Carolina Press, 2002.

Taylor, Dale. *The Writer's Guide to Everyday Life in Colonial America*. Cincinnati: Writer's Digest Books, 1997.

Truro town records.

CHAPTER 3: THE SETTLER-FARMER BECOMES FISHERMAN-WHALER

The Reverend James Freeman was the first to write a description of Truro and how its people made their living. He was one of three distinguished visitors in the dozen years between 1794 and 1807 who wrote about the town. A Boston minister, he led the first Unitarian church in America and was a founder of the Massachusetts Historical Society. Six years after he published his topographical description of Truro, Timothy Dwight, president of Yale, wrote letters about his visit, and in 1807 Edward Augustus Kendall, a prolific British writer, observed the life of fishermen and whalingmen in Truro during his travels in New England.

Barber, John Warner. *Historical Collections...Every Town in Massachusetts*. 3 vols. Worcester: Lazell, 1839 and 1844.

Child, Mrs. (Lydia Maria). *The American Frugal Housewife, Dedicated to Those Who Are Not Ashamed of Economy*. 12th ed. Boston: Carter, Hendee & Co., 1832. Reprint. Boston: Applewood Books, N.d. Advice on how to raise children, prepare food, furnish a home, clean everything in the household, cure major and minor illnesses, and keep healthy.

Cobbett, William. *A Year's Residence in the United States of America*. New York: 1818.

Dwight, Timothy. *Travels in New England and New York*. Vol. 3. New Haven: Timothy Dwight, 1822. Reprint with notes by Barbara Miller Solomon. Cambridge MA: Harvard Press, 1969.

Dyer, John B. "Historical Address." In *Report of the Officers of the Town of Truro for the Year Ending Dec. 31, 1909*. Truro MA: 1910.

Earle, Alice Morse. *Home Life in Colonial Days*. New York: Grosset & Dunlop, 1898. Reprint Stockbridge MA: Berkshire Traveler Press, 1974.
———. *Stage-Coach and Tavern Days*. New York: Macmillan Company, 1930.

[Freeman, the Reverend James.] "A Topographical Description of Truro in the County of Barnstable, 1794." In *Collections of the Massachusetts Historical Society*. Vol. 3, series one. Boston: n.d. Reprint. New York: Johnson Reprint Corporation, n.d. F. W. P. Greenwood identifies Freeman as the author of accounts of towns on Cape Cod.

Kendall, Edward Augustus. *Travels Through the Northern Parts of the United States in the Years 1807 and 1808*. New York: Riley, 1809.

Larkin, Jack. *The Reshaping of Everyday Life 1790–1840*. New York: Harper & Row, 1988. An excellent survey and bibliography.

Nylander, Jane C. "Provision for Daughters: The Accounts of Samuel Lane." In *House and Home, the Annual Proceedings of the Dublin Seminar for New England Folklife*. Boston University: 1988.

Quinn, William P. *The Saltworks of Historic Cape Cod*. Orleans MA: Parnassus Imprints, 1993.

Rich, Shebnah. *Truro—Cape Cod or Land Marks and Sea Marks*. Boston: D. Lothrop & Company, 1883. Reprint. Rutland VT: Charles E. Tuttle Company, 1988. See chapter XIX, "How They Lived" and pages 256-7, 441 and 559. While intended primarily as a history of Truro from its beginnings to the 1880s, Rich's book includes some details on everyday life from his own lifetime, from his experience fishing and from stories he heard from his parents' and grandparents' generations.

SOURCES

Smith, Barbara Clark. *After the Revolution: The Smithsonian History of Everyday Life in the Eighteenth Century*. New York: Pantheon Books, 1985. Detailed descriptions of households and family life in three towns in Massachusetts, Delaware and Virginia.

Thoreau, Henry David. *Cape Cod*. Boston: Ticknor and Fields, 1865. Reprint, with an introduction by Robert Finch. Hyannis MA: Parnassus Imprints, 1984.

Weld, Isaac. *Travels Through the States of North America, and the Provinces of Upper and Lower Canada*. 2 vols. London, 1807.

Wolf, Stephanie Grauman. *As Various as Their Land: The Everyday Lives of Eighteenth Century Americans*. New York: HarperCollins, 1993.

CHAPTER 4: THE YANKEES AND PORTUGUESE OF VICTORIAN TRURO

Although American historians generally consider the Victorian Age in the United States to extend from the 1870s to the start of World War I in 1914, this account of everyday life in Victorian Truro focuses on the 1890s, the mid-point. The decades that follow are covered in detail by Anthony L. Marshall in his memoir of his youth in Truro.

Brennan, Susan W. and Diana Worthington. *Images of America: Truro*. Charleston SC: Arcadia Publishing, 2002. A collection of photographs of Truro, most of them in the twentieth century, including weir fishing, the railroad and Charlie Snow's road maintenance equipment.

Brewer, Priscilla J. *From Fireplace to Cookstove: Technology and the Domestic Ideal in America*. Syracuse NY: Syracuse University Press, 2000. The best of several books on the impact of the cast iron cookstove on America.

Crosby, Katharine. *Blue-water Men and Other Cape Codders*. New York: Macmillan Company, 1947.

Deyo, Simeon L., ed. *History of Barnstable County, Massachusetts, 1620– 1890*. New York: H.W. Blake & Co., 1890. Fourteen of the twenty-eight chapters are signed by special contributors but not the chapter on Truro. Whoever wrote it knew all about the stores.

Digges, Jeremiah [Josef Berger]. *Cape Cod Pilot*. New York: Viking Press, 1937. Reprint. MIT Press, 1969.

Drake, Samuel Adams. *Nooks and Corners of the New England Coast*. New York: Harper & Brothers, 1875. Includes drawings of Highland Light and Pond Village.

Halter, Marilyn. *Between Race and Ethnicity: Cape Verdean Immigrants, 1860–1965*. Urbana and Chicago: University of Illinois Press, 1993.

Marshall, Anthony L. *Truro, Cape Cod, As I Knew It*. N.p. 1974. Reprint. Truro Historical Society, 1987. A memoir of everyday life in Truro from about 1910 to 1920. He was eight years old in 1910, left Truro in 1920 and returned more than fifty years later to write his memoir. It is full of homely details about the town's people and places, including a full chapter on the Portuguese.

Massachusetts Bureau of Statistics of Labor. *Twenty-Seventh Annual Report*. Boston: 1897. The report includes census figures and lengthy, firsthand accounts of the economic life in Truro, Wellfleet and Provincetown in the 1890s, with special focus on the immigration of "Western Islanders." The report classifies as Western Islanders immigrants (and their children) from the Cape Verde Islands, off the west coast of Africa, and from the Azores, off the west coast of Portugal, even while noting that only the Azores were generally called the Western Islands. Both island groups were Portuguese colonies. Marshall does not call them Western Islanders, but refers to them briefly three times as "Cape Verdeans" (pp 41, 45 and 70). Some of these were undoubtedly of Afro-Portuguese descent. Rich has only one sentence on the Portuguese, who were beginning to move into Truro in the 1870s and 1880s when he was writing his history of Truro. The Collins farm on South Pamet, he says, "passed into the hand of strangers from the Azores." (Town and census records do not make clear how many immigrants came to the Outer Cape from which islands.) "Portuguese" seems the most appropriate descriptor for the immigrants even though none or very few had ancestors in Portugal, since Marshall, who says he was of Portuguese ancestry, used that term throughout his chapter on "The Portuguese in Town" (pp 73-82).

Nason, the Reverend Elias. *A Gazetteer of the State of Massachusetts*. Boston: B.B. Russell, 1874.

SOURCES

Pap, Leo. *The Portuguese-Americans*. Boston: Twayne Publishers, 1981. Includes references to the Outer Cape and the complexities of the racial-ethnic identities.

Perry, E.G. *A Trip Around Cape Cod...Plymouth*. 3rd ed. Boston and Monument Beach MA: N.p. 1898. Includes his visit to Truro and visit with Aunt Hepsey, plus many photographs of the town.

Provincetown Advocate. "My Pamet" column by Tom Kane. August 24, 1978. For Charlie Snow's tale.

Quarles, Hillary. "Cultural Landscape Inventory: Summary Report, Pamet Cranberry Bog." Typescript. N.p. 1995. Prepared for the Cape Cod National Seashore.

Resident and Business Directory of Cape Cod, Massachusetts, 1901, Comprising the Towns of Provincetown, Truro, Wellfleet, Eastham, Orleans and Brewster. South Framingham MA: A.E. Foss Publishing Co., 1901.

Rich, Shebnah. *Truro—Cape Cod or Land Marks and Sea Marks*. Boston: D. Lothrop & Company, 1883. Reprint. Rutland VT: Charles E. Tuttle Company, 1988.

Schlereth, Thomas J. *Victorian America: Transformations in Everyday Life, 1876–1915*. New York: HarperCollins Publishers, 1991. A detailed, lively survey of the commonplace experiences, occupations, material goods, and life styles of Americans during the period.

Small, Isaac M. ("Mort"). *Just a Little About the Lower Cape, Personal and Otherwise*. Middleborough MA: Nemasket Press, 1922.
———. *True Stories of Cape Cod*. New Bedford MA: Reynolds, 1934.

Sutherland, Daniel E. *The Expansion of Everyday Life, 1860–1876*. New York: Harper & Row, 1989.

Truro town records.

Vorse, Mary Heaton. *Time and the Town: A Provincetown Chronicle*. N.p., 1942. Reprint with corrections. Provincetown: Cape Cod Pilgrim Memorial Association, 1990. Vorse, who arrived in Provincetown around 1907, wrote about her appreciation of the Portuguese.

Index

About the Author

Richard F. Whalen, author and lecturer, has served on various civic committees in Truro, including the Finance Committee and the Truro Conservation Trust. He was the lead writer of Truro's first town charter. He has published articles in many publications, including *The Historical Journal of Massachusetts* and *Harper's Magazine*.